D1155768

Undocumented and in College

Copyright © 2017 Fordham University Press

All rights reserved. No part of this publication may be reproduced, stored in a retrieval system, or transmitted in any form or by any means—electronic, mechanical, photocopy, recording, or any other—except for brief quotations in printed reviews, without the prior permission of the publisher.

Fordham University Press has no responsibility for the persistence or accuracy of URLs for external or third-party Internet websites referred to in this publication and does not guarantee that any content on such websites is, or will remain, accurate or appropriate.

Fordham University Press also publishes its books in a variety of electronic formats. Some content that appears in print may not be available in electronic books.

Visit us online at www.fordhampress.com.

Library of Congress Cataloging-in-Publication Data

Names: Jones, Terry-Ann, 1977– editor. | Nichols, Laura, editor.
Title: Undocumented and in college : students and institutions in
    a climate of national hostility / Terry-Ann Jones and Laura
    Nichols, editors.
Description: First edition. | New York : Fordham University Press,
    [2017] | Includes bibliographical references and index.
Identifiers: LCCN 2016051378 | ISBN 9780823276165
    (cloth : alk. paper) | ISBN 9780823276172 (pbk. : alk. paper)
Subjects: LCSH: Illegal aliens—Education (Higher)—United States. |
    Illegal aliens—Education (Higher)—Government policy—United
    States. | Universities and colleges—Residence requirements—
    United States. | Jesuit universities and colleges—United States.
Classification: LCC LC3731 .U528 2017 | DDC 378.19820973—dc23
LC record available at https://lccn.loc.gov/2016051378

Printed in the United States of America

19 18 17   5 4 3 2 1

First edition

Contents

Preface

This book is the result of a four-year study of the experiences of colleges and college students in the United States who are traversing higher education while undocumented. The chapters in the book explore how the situation of such immigrants has changed over time and what the current legal challenges and opportunities are for this growing population of students. A description of this Ford Foundation–funded study can be found in the Introduction. While many of the chapter authors worked on the original study, additional scholars have been included to help to add context and to update our findings with current college practices.

As co-editors of this book, we were both part of the social science research team that interviewed staff, faculty, and students and analyzed the various types of data collected to gain an understanding of how institutions have responded and adapted to having undocumented students on their campuses. The research took place, as is the case now, at a time with high migration rates around the world and when immigration politics and policy are extremely contested issues that bring out strong, often hostile emotional reactions, very divergent policy views and proposals, and the potential for human rights abuses. The study provides the opportunity to also look at the role of another institutional actor in the debates: religious organizations, namely, the responses of the twenty-eight colleges in the U.S. Catholic Jesuit higher education network. This context provides another layer of analysis: the role of these mission-driven institutions in responding and reacting to this contested issue. Studying this particular system of schools is extremely useful for a study such as this because the earliest schools in the network were founded to provide schooling to the new immigrants of that time, namely, Catholic Italian and Irish first generation immigrants.

The strategic research design of the study allowed for the opportunity to understand all twenty-eight schools, and to use a case study approach to explore specific practices and experiences at six of those institutions on the West Coast, in the Midwest, and on the East Coast. While some areas of the United States tend to attract immigrants from particular parts of the world, we found that the challenges for students and institutional responses were similar across the United States.

The authors are all faculty and staff who currently work or have worked at these institutions. As such we have had personal experiences interacting with and learning from these extremely high-achieving students as they attempt to manage the complicated realities of being undocumented while considering the United States the only home that they have truly known. As faculty members on the East Coast (Terry-Ann) and West Coast (Laura), we have seen students who have excelled in high school, earned competitive scholarships to attend our expensive institutions, struggled to fit in and afford college and support their families, excelled in their majors, and then graduated to uncertain futures, working at jobs that severely under-utilize their skills and abilities. We also have seen our institutions struggle to fulfill their missions to provide an equal educational experience for all students, while limited by federal policies and larger societal attitudes about immigration and immigrants.

While the study and our experiences allow us to see, close up, how institutions and students deal with the issues related to being undocumented on a day-to-day basis, this book puts these experiences in a larger context. It provides the opportunity to consider how immigration policy has affected undocumented students over time and how colleges as institutional agents have responded along with and sometimes in opposition to these larger societal forces. As such, the experiences of students and institutions chronicled in these chapters can be extremely instructive in informing future policy initiatives that must eventually grapple with the reality of having so many people without authorization working in our low-paying economy and attending our public schools. While there are no easy fixes, this study is further evidence of the opportunity and potential of finding a compassionate way forward that can also be cost-effective given the national resources already invested in young immigrants who are striving to realize an American Dream that appears to be more and more elusive.

Terry-Ann Jones and Laura Nichols

Undocumented and in College

Introduction

MELISSA QUAN

Valuing education has been a defining characteristic of the Society of Jesus since its inception in 1540. Saint Ignatius of Loyola, the founder of the Society of Jesus, intended Jesuit education to be free and open to all social classes and saw it as an important contribution to the "common good" of society (O'Malley, 2000). Before long, the Jesuits created a worldwide network of colleges and universities anchored in a humanistic education and a common concern for the moral development of students. At present, there are over 180 Jesuit colleges and universities worldwide and hundreds more primary and secondary schools.

American Jesuit higher education began with the founding of Georgetown University, the oldest U.S. Catholic and Jesuit University, in 1789 and has stretched to the founding of Wheeling Jesuit University in 1954. At present, there are twenty-eight Jesuit colleges and universities spread across various regions of the United States.[1] A pivotal moment for Jesuit education around the world came with the 32nd General Congregation of the Society of Jesus, a gathering of Jesuit leaders from around the world for the purpose of discussing how the Society of Jesus was to respond to Vatican II's call for the transformation of the Catholic Church (Kolvenbach, 2000). A significant outcome of the 32nd General Congregation was an explicit commitment to the "promotion of justice" through education—including student formation, teaching, faculty research, and service (Kolvenbach, 2000). In a well-known address at Santa Clara University in 2000, Fr. Peter Hans Kolvenbach, then Superior General of the Society of Jesus said,

> Students in the course of their formation, must let the gritty reality of this world into their lives, so they can learn to feel it, think about it critically, respond to its suffering, and engage it constructively. They

should learn to perceive, think, judge, choose, and act for the rights of others, especially the disadvantaged and the oppressed (p. 155).

He goes on to say about faculty research,

> Every discipline, beyond its necessary specialization, must engage with human society . . . cultivating moral concern about how people ought to live together . . . All professors . . . are in contact with the world. But no point of view is ever neutral or value free. By preference, by option, our Jesuit point of view is that of the poor (p. 157).

As Catholic institutions, Jesuit schools are deeply rooted in Catholic social teaching (CST). CST refers to modern teachings of the Church relative to social life. These teachings are often in the form of papal encyclicals or major church documents such as those put out by bishop conferences. From these documents, major themes have emerged, which make up CST and are often referred to as principles (Brigham, 2013; Henriot, DeBerri, and Schultheis, 2001). An important and overarching theme of CST is the *dignity of the human person*, which flows from the belief that each person is an expression of God's creativity and that the rights bestowed by God apply to all human beings equally: "we have all been created in the image and likeness of God, we are all primarily social by nature, and the goods of the earth have been made for all to enjoy" (Tampe, 1995). In addition, the theme of *solidarity* leads us to recognize our global and local responsibility to help one another and is based on the belief that the well-being of one person is connected to the well-being of another (Henriot, DeBerri, and Schultheis, 2001). Flowing from these beliefs in the dignity of every human person and global solidarity, the church's view on immigration transcends nationality, ethnicity, economics, and so on. Thus, in the U.S. context, these responsibilities to protect human dignity and live in solidarity are not to be restricted to U.S. citizens but rather extended to all men and women (Tampe, 1995).

Moving beyond the intellectual understanding of the role of religion, Jaqueline Maria Hagan reveals the deeply personal, human interactions that flow from beliefs, such as those in the Catholic tradition, that Jesus was the first migrant and is present in the faces of contemporary migrants.[2] In her extensive study of the phases of migration—pre-departure, journey, and integration—she documents the important role of faith and religion in the migration experience. Through in-depth interviews with over two hundred migrants who journeyed from Latin America to the United States, as well as support persons working within faith-based institutions along the migrant pathways, she uncovers the role of faith in people's decision to migrate, their ability to persevere through the journey, and their integration experience. The transcendence of faith over borders is reflected in the ways that religious organizations support migrants and the way migrants reciprocate that support throughout their journey.

Jesuit institutions—colleges and universities, high schools, parishes, Provinces, the Jesuit Conference, and affiliated organizations such as the Ignatian Solidarity Network—have long been vocal in their advocacy for immigrant rights, particularly undocumented children. In the 2010 Association of Jesuit Colleges and Universities (AJCU) mission and apostolate statement, the U.S. Jesuit presidents reaffirmed their commitment to "continuing the historic mission of educating first generation students . . . [and to] prioritize the education of these often vulnerable and underserved students." Following, in 2013 the Jesuit Provincials sent letters to the president of the United States and to all members of Congress, calling them to take up comprehensive immigration reform. The reform that the Provincials called for included a path to citizenship, protective employment structures, and family reunification, as well as policies to promote fair economic relationships and exchanges with countries most impacted by migration.[3] Additionally, many Jesuit institutions and affiliates have joined with the U.S. Conference of Catholic Bishops, the Interfaith Immigration Coalition, and the Association of Catholic Colleges and Universities to develop a united, faith-based voice to advocate for comprehensive immigration reform and humane approaches to addressing the immigration crises.[4]

So, when a program director at the Ford Foundation suggested to Fr. Jeffrey P. von Arx, S.J., President of Fairfield University, that there was a lack of leadership and moral voice within higher education regarding the challenges facing undocumented students, and that the Jesuit network of institutions across the United States was uniquely poised to respond, it was no surprise that Fr. von Arx was ready and prepared to take on the challenge. The result was the *Immigrant Students National Position Paper*, a study of the situation of undocumented students at the twenty-eight Jesuit colleges and universities in the United States and the institutional practices that affect those students. The research was conducted over two years (2010–2012) by legal and social science research teams at Fairfield University in Connecticut, Santa Clara University in California, and Loyola University in Chicago. Each of the three lead research universities paired with another AJCU campus in their respective region to do case studies and an in-depth look at the context and situation on six campuses in three distinct U.S. regions: Northeast, Midwest, and West. Together, the six institutions represented the breadth and depth of Jesuit education— from a research university with graduate programs, law school, and a medical school, to an all-undergraduate university with a large number of commuter and part-time students. A survey was also conducted at all twenty-eight schools across the United States.

The Project

The *Immigrant Students National Position Paper* was implemented in two phases: the research phase and the dissemination phase. The goals of the overall project were (1) to provide presidential leadership in higher education regarding undocumented students; (2) to initiate and sustain a dialogue with the twenty-eight U.S. Jesuit colleges and universities around the topic of undocumented students with a special focus on six schools; (3) to design and implement a mixed-methods research study to understand the legal contexts, attitudes, and current practices, issues, and challenges for AJCU institutions in serving students who are undocumented; and (4) to develop and disseminate a white paper that would summarize the research findings and provide a moral argument for serving undocumented students.

Methodology

The research, conducted between June 2010 and July 2012, employed a mixed methods research model that included an online survey of faculty, staff, and administrators across the twenty-eight U.S. Jesuit colleges and universities as well as in-depth structured interviews with faculty, staff, and students at six Jesuit colleges and universities as well as community advocates. The presidents of the twenty-eight U.S. Jesuit colleges and universities each identified a "contact person" on their campus. This person served as a resource and liaison to the research team and helped to identify survey respondents and interviewees. Survey respondents included "key staff" on the campuses most likely to come into contact with undocumented students. These individuals ranged from admissions counselors to campus ministers, diversity officers, financial aid personnel, and faculty. These "key staff members" were also among those who participated in the in-depth interviews as well as those who helped to identify and engage the participation of undocumented student interviewees.

Prior to beginning the research, each of the three lead research schools obtained approval from their respective Institutional Review Boards. Additionally, the research team obtained a Certificate of Confidentiality from the National Institute of Child and Human Development. This certificate provided additional protection to the researchers and the universities from any pressures to reveal the identity of any of the students, staff, or community members who participated in the research.

Survey

The survey, conducted online through "Key Survey," was designed to explore practices and attitudes toward undocumented students at all twenty-eight Jesuit colleges and universities across the country. An e-mail list of approximately 200 key staff members (admissions, financial aid, student services, and so forth) representing all twenty-eight institutions was compiled, and all were invited to complete the survey online; a total of 110 responded. The survey questions included both fixed-choice answers and open-ended questions.

Interviews

A total of forty-seven interviews were completed with staff and faculty at six universities—two institutions in the West, two in the Midwest, and two in the East. Interviews were conducted by members of the social research team.

In-depth personal interviews were also conducted with twenty-five undergraduate students who were undocumented at the time of the interview and were enrolled in one of the six case study institutions at the time of the study. The interviews explored students' journey through the admissions process, financial aid issues, and their experiences on campus. The students were also asked to describe their family backgrounds. All students interviewed were primarily raised in the U.S., most arriving in the country from as young as forty days to no older than nine years; two came as teenagers. Many had younger siblings who were born in the U.S. and were U.S. citizens. Students were provided with a twenty-five-dollar gift certificate for their participation.

A limited number of interviews were additionally conducted with community advocates, who often play a key role in encouraging undocumented students to apply and enroll at Jesuit institutions. These individuals included high school teachers and guidance counselors as well as parish priests.

Interviews with faculty, staff, students, and community advocates were audio recorded, anatomized, transcribed, and then qualitatively analyzed with NVivo® software. Each interviewee signed a consent form before the interviews began. All individual interview information remained strictly confidential and personal identifiers were removed. To protect their confidentiality, each interviewee was assigned an identification number and interview transcripts were stored on a secure server. Efforts were made in the white paper to select quotes that could not be used to identify any one person.

Dissemination

The research team was awarded a second grant from the Ford Foundation to facilitate dissemination of the research findings between September 2012 and June 2013. The findings were compiled as a 36-page white paper titled *Immigration: Undocumented Students in Higher Education* along with supporting materials including a Frequently Asked Questions document, an Executive Summary, a Press Release, and a Statement of Support signed by twenty-five of twenty-eight Association of Jesuit Colleges and Universities presidents. The report and supplementary materials were shared across twenty-eight Jesuit colleges and universities across the nation and circulated through the network of American Catholic colleges and universities, public higher education institutions, religious and secular NGOs, various media outlets, and policy-makers and legislators in Washington, D.C.

A key element of the dissemination phase included a public presentation on Capitol Hill, Washington, D.C. In February 2013, the research team convened in the Russell Senate Office Building with a diverse audience of over 150 people, including over 55 students from seven Jesuit colleges and universities across the U.S; 12 AJCU presidents, representatives from a number of Washington-based NGOs, and representatives from several congressional offices.

Following the event in Washington, a web page was created to host the research findings and supplementary materials and to serve as a repository for resources related to undocumented students in higher education.[5]

Immigrants and Jesuit Higher Education

While much of the public discourse on immigration focuses on undocumented immigrants working in the low-income economy, it is not as widely known that undocumented students can and do legally attend tertiary educational institutions. Each year, it is estimated that sixty-five thousand undocumented students graduate from high school, but only 5 to 10 percent go on to post-secondary education.[6] While the implications of this vast majority of undocumented students missing the opportunity of post-secondary education are unknown, based on what we do know about the value of higher education to financial stability and well-being we can assume that implications include the exacerbation of unemployment, under-employment, poverty, and inequality. For those undocumented students who do enter higher education, this project uncovered some of the challenges that the students face at Jesuit institutions.

The overarching purpose of the *Immigrant Student National Position Paper* was to create a model for other institutions of higher education based on the idea that,

> If the whole Jesuit system of higher education in the United States were to become fully engaged in the challenges and issues of undocumented students, other colleges and universities could be emboldened with their own unique senses of mission and identity to exercise new models of leadership in this area of immigration.[7]

Researchers took an in-depth look at the practices, attitudes, challenges, and opportunities relative to undocumented students in the twenty-eight

U.S. Jesuit colleges and universities. The project also explored the roles of the institutions as well as other actors in facilitating the students' enrollment and matriculation and post-graduate success from moral, legal, and social perspectives. Other research questions included: How do current federal and state laws and practices impact the undocumented student's college experience? How can a morally committed network of Jesuit higher education institutions join together to collaboratively support the human dignity of undocumented students who find themselves adrift in a world hostile to their future because of a past they did not choose for themselves?

Through its research and broad support, this study sought to explain the current situation and practices at Jesuit institutions and examine the concerns and perceptions of students, staff, and faculty on this critical issue. Both ongoing problems and successful institutional practices have been unearthed, and the researchers recommended developing a collaborative model of new practices that will support undocumented students in these unsettling and turbulent times.

This book on undocumented students at Jesuit institutions of higher education in the United States expands upon the work of the *Immigration Student National Position Paper*. With this foundational introduction, the book continues with a chapter by Terry-Ann Jones, who discusses major theoretical approaches to immigration and its intersection with educational institutions, and underscores the inadequacies of dominant theories in accounting for the experiences of undocumented students. The plight of undocumented adolescents and the roadblocks that they face as they exit the public school system and attempt to further their education has gained public awareness as support for the Development, Relief, and Education for Alien Minors (DREAM) Act has gained recognition and momentum.

In the second chapter, Kurt Schlichting guides readers through the history of migration to the U.S. starting in the 1500s and discusses the role of religious institutions, including Jesuit colleges starting in the early 1800s, in providing for the needs of recent immigrants. Ana Siscar and Sahng-Ah Yoo present an overview of the impact of historical and recent developments in immigration law on undocumented students' access and success in higher education. In the third chapter specific topics discussed include the legality of admission in postsecondary institutions, lack of access to federal financial aid, unfounded prohibition from access to institutional aid, the various legislations on in-state tuition fees and state financial aid, inability to pursue a profession, and the Deferred Action for Childhood Arrivals (DACA) program. In sum, it covers the salient legal developments that opened up opportunities in K-college education as well as those that raised barriers.

In chapter four, Michael Canaris explores the theological and moral dimensions of educating persons who are not recognized as citizens, along with the wider applicability and relevance of such principles to people and institutions of all faith traditions, and none.

Laura Nichols and Maria Guzmán present the key findings from students in chapter five, where they highlight the main themes that students raised about being an undergraduate student who is also undocumented. The diversity of students' experiences is underscored here. Suzanna Klaf and Katherine Kaufka Walts discuss the research findings from the institutional perspective in chapter six, which presents the results of the survey data and in-depth interviews with members of the institutions' staff. Laura Nichols and Terry-Ann Jones conclude the book by addressing some of the questions that were raised throughout the project, and with a discussion of the implications of the research findings for future undocumented students, higher education institutions, and U.S. policy.

Conclusion

To some degree, Jesuit higher education has lost its special connection with new immigrants due in large part to the rising costs of higher education and resulting changes in undergraduate and graduate student profiles. This disconnect with the immigrant roots of Jesuit higher education is exacerbated when immigration policy and issues related to large numbers of undocumented persons living in the U.S. are hot-button political issues and lead university constituents to question why institutional aid should be awarded to undocumented students while there are those with U.S citizenship still in need. Nonetheless, the system of Jesuit higher education in this country mirrors in many ways the breadth and diversity of private higher education in the United States. What sets Jesuit schools apart is their collective reputation for promoting the common good through their approaches to serving students and the community and through the incorporation of Catholic social teaching in their educational projects.

The history of Jesuit higher education in the United States is inextricably linked to first- and second-generation immigrant populations.

Additionally, Jesuit institutions have a shared commitment to promoting the common good through education. Thus, supporting undocumented students and serving as a leading voice on issues of immigration in the United States is closely tied to the mission of Jesuit education. A leading hypothesis of this research study was that, if the whole Jesuit system of higher education in the U.S. were to become fully engaged in the challenges and issues of undocumented students, other colleges and universities might be emboldened with their own unique senses of mission and identity to exercise new models of leadership in this area of immigration. The study aimed to present a deeper understanding of the complex lives of undocumented students. The hope was that deeper understanding would generate more public compassion as well as help guide institutions in ethically providing the resources necessary for students to succeed and encourage consistent policy that allows for the talents, skills, and gifts of undocumented students to be shared once they graduate from college.

Notes

1. See http://www.ajcunet.edu/institutions for more information on the U.S. Jesuit colleges and universities.

2. Hagan, *Migration Miracle*.

3. See http://nyknenprov.jesuits.org/hidden?PAGE=DTN-20141114025238.

4. See USCCB's Justice for Immigrants campaign: http://www .justiceforimmigrants.org and http://www.interfaithimmigration.org.

5. See www.fairfield.edu/immigrantstudent.

6. A. Russell, *State Policies Regarding Undocumented College Students: A Narrative of Unresolved Issues, Ongoing Debate and Missed Opportunities* (Washington, D.C.: American Association of State Colleges and Universities, 2011).

7. Emphasis added. "Immigrant Student National Position Paper: Report on Findings," January 2013. Retrieved from http://www.fairfield.edu/media /fairfielduniversitywebsite/documents/academic/cfpl_immigration_report.pdf.

References

Association of Jesuit Colleges and Universities. *The Jesuit, Catholic Mission of U.S. Jesuit Colleges and Universities*. Washington D.C., 2010.

Brigham, E. M. *See, Judge, Act: Catholic Social Teaching and Service Learning*. Winona, Minn.: Anselm Academic, 2013.

Fairfield University, Loyola University Chicago, and Santa Clara University Legal and Social Research Teams. "Immigrant Students National Position Paper. (2013). http://www.fairfield.edu/media/fairfielduniversitywebsite /documents/academic/cfpl_immigration_summary.pdf.

Hagan, Jacqueline Maria. *Migration Miracle: Faith, Hope, and Meaning on the Undocumented Journey.* Cambridge, Mass.: Harvard University Press, 2008.

Henriot, P. J., E. P. DeBerri, and M. J. Schultheis, *Catholic Social Teaching: Our Best Kept Secret* (10th ed.). New York: Orbis Books; and Washington, D.C.: Center of Concern, 2001.

Kolvenbach, P. H., S.J. "The Service of Faith and the Promotion of Justice in American Jesuit Higher Education." In *A Jesuit Education Reader* (2000). Retrieved from https://books.google.com/books?hl=en&lr=&id =uvFn6N2dA3YC&oi=fnd&pg=PA144&dq=Kolvenbach,+P.+H. +%282000%29.+The+service+of+faith+and+the+promotion+of+justice +in+American+Jesuit+higher+education.+A+Jesuit+Education+Reader. &ots=16fzWfSOhB&sig=mXdfMAzq7-9dPEzqJQALGtKV5bg#v =onepage&q&f=false.

O'Malley, J. W. "How the First Jesuits Became Involved in Education." In *The Jesuit Ratio Studiorum: 400th Anniversary Perspectives*, edited by V. J. Duminuco. New York: Fordham University Press, 2000.

Tampe, Luis, S.J. *The Lifeboat and the Banquet: Two Images for Contemplating Immigrant Human Rights.* Jesuit Conference USA. Washington, D.C., 1995.

1   Theoretical and Conceptual Considerations for the Study of Undocumented College Students

TERRY-ANN JONES

Introduction

Developing a model through which to understand the reasons for migration has long been central to the field of migration studies, and the scholarship that has emerged to better understand this common human activity has contributed to this effort. The movement of human beings across regions predates the establishment of political borders, yet scholars still struggle to understand the process through a comprehensive theoretical approach. Scholars of migration theory often lament that there is no single, comprehensive theory of international migration that reflects the myriad contemporary processes of migration. I would argue that there should not be a single, comprehensive theoretical approach to such diverse, dynamic processes in which both the players and their realities are so widely divergent, even if they hail from similar countries or regions. Instead, scholars have developed several varying and often complementary approaches that define, explain, and predict processes of international migration. This chapter reviews the major theoretical approaches to international migration and considers their use as a tool to explain the dynamics surrounding the migration processes, meanings of citizenship, race/ethnicity, racism, stigmatization, and other challenges that undocumented youth encounter in interacting with institutions, particularly in their pursuit of a tertiary-level education.

Classical Theories of International Migration

Although theories of international migration have evolved as scholars have debated the priorities and considerations that drive the migration process, Ravenstein's "laws of migration"[1] is commonly cited as the starting point for the development of migration theory. Ravenstein developed a set of governing principles related to migration, among which he theorized that migration is primarily caused by economic factors.

Lee's concept of the push-pull theory of migration is similarly fundamental to the development of contemporary theories of migration that explain the decision-making process, as the decision to migrate involves consideration of the characteristics of the home country that individuals and families try to escape (push factors) and factors that are attractive in the receiving country (pull factors).[2] About three-quarters of the undocumented population of the United States are Latinos, and the majority of undocumented students were born in Latin America, particularly Central America. Accordingly, the push factors that propel their families to the United States are likely to include poverty, political instability, and increasingly prevalent gang-motivated crime and violence, all of which are pervasive in the parts of Latin America that are the major sending countries of undocumented immigrants in the United States. That the five countries with the highest murder rates in the world are all in Latin America (Honduras, Venezuela, Belize, El Salvador, and Guatemala)[3] is undoubtedly related to the urgency with which people emigrate from these countries, even without the documentation that they require for legal status. From the standpoint of the receiving country, the relative political and economic stability and the prospects for upward socioeconomic mobility serve as attractive pull factors, even when discerning migrants consider the risk of entering and living in the United States without legal immigration status. Further, the breakdown of immigration policy post-1986 in the United States combined with heightened security efforts post-9/11 has resulted in immigration policies and practices that are at best ambiguous and at worst conflictual, leaving individuals and families at the mercy of local sentiment and constantly changing political power.[4] It is on this basis of contemplating the risks and benefits associated with migration that the following theories of international migration are based.

Contemporary Theories of International Migration

Building on Lee's model of a decision-making process that weighs the potential benefits of migration against the potential costs, other theories of migration have emerged, many of which assume that an individual makes a rational decision based on her or his best interests, or perhaps the best interests of their children or other family members. Other models are based on macroeconomic factors and structural patterns that are beyond the control of individual migrants. The neoclassical economics approach is based on the assumption that transnational discrepancies in labor supply, demand, and wages serve as major motivating factors for migration. Migrants, according to this approach, leave countries with high unemployment, high labor supply, and low wages in favor of countries with lower unemployment, higher labor demand, and higher wages. The assumption that migration essentially serves to improve the economic conditions of migrants has, however, attracted much criticism, as it does not account for the myriad other factors that encourage people to leave their home countries, or the macroeconomic factors that individuals do not determine.

Both the world-systems approach and the dual labor market approach consider the macroeconomic and structural factors that influence migration decisions. According to the world-systems approach, migration is the result of inequities between states and as long as those inequities persist, the flow of people will continue from poor countries with limited global influence, or "periphery" countries, to the wealthy, dominant, "core" countries. In contrast to the world-systems analysis' emphasis on the power dynamics between countries, the dual or segmented labor market approach considers the conditions of the receiving country's domestic labor market. The duality or segmentation of the labor market refers to the tendency in migrant-receiving countries for some jobs to be relegated to a secondary status, marked by lower wages, lower skill level, and less security. For example in the United States, positions in agricultural labor, slaughterhouses and meat processing, landscaping, and domestic work are often stigmatized in this way. The consequence of the stigmatization of some segments of the labor market is that these "secondary" types of jobs become unattractive to the U.S.-born, which then limits the availability of labor, creating a demand for foreign labor. This demand stimulates the impetus to migrate.

The new household economics of migration is grounded in a similar assumption as the neoclassical economics approach, that migration is a response to global differentials in the supply and demand of labor and capital.[5] However, in this model the cost-benefit analysis of the possible risks that the migration process might entail versus potential economic gains considers the family or household rather than just the individual.

In this context, the expectation is that the decision, the costs, and the benefits are all shared by the family or household. For example, it is not uncommon for parents to migrate without their children, leaving them in the care of family members while they seek employment abroad. Leaving the children behind eases the difficult process of obtaining employment, caretaking, and housing, but the migrant then has the obligation to support not only herself and her children who remain in the home country, but also caregivers and possibly other family members. As such, the later migration of children who are or become undocumented is likely to affect not only the individual child or her parents, but also a broader network that could include the extended family, and members of the family or household may incur expenses through the process. The migration of undocumented children ought not be reduced to only economic motivations; rather, an understanding of the significance of kinship networks in the decision to migrate, as well as the difficulties or lack of opportunities in the home country that would make the risk of undocumented status a more attractive option than staying at home, are fundamental to developing an understanding of the needs, fears, and challenges that new immigrant students in the United States face, especially their anxieties over protecting their family members. The new household economics model also recognizes that wage differentials are not necessary for migration to occur; there are other risks and benefits such as personal safety and educational opportunities for family members that are also considered.

To distinguish the new household economics of migration from the neoclassical approach, Porumbescu underscores the divergent ways in which each of the two approaches perceives return migration.[6] Because the neoclassical economics approach posits that migration occurs in order to improve wages and economic standing, return migration suggests a failure to attain this upward mobility. On the other hand, the new household economics of migration prioritizes the family and/or household, so return migration suggests that the migrant has attained the desired goals of migration and the return is an indicator of success.

Although the family commitments that are embedded in the new household economics of migration suggest that parents carefully weigh the costs and benefits of migrating with children who will be without legal migration status, parents are often criticized for their role in the predicament of undocumented children and youth. Using the example of the perception of asylum-seeking children and their parents in Norway, Engebrigtsen contends that the generally negative way in which they are perceived by the Norwegian public reflects cultural biases.[7] The parent-child relationship is assumed to be based on care and nurturing of the child by the parent according to Norwegian standards of parenting, and placing a child in the precarious position of being an undocumented immigrant is deemed to be contradictory to these standards. However, Engebrigtsen argues that based on the perspectives of some of the countries of origin of unaccompanied minors who arrive in Norway, the child can from an early age express care and nurturing for his or her family through the process of migration, which can lead to prosperity for the family. In other words, assumptions on the part of receiving societies that undocumented children have been harmed by their families fail to consider the nuanced ways in which care is expressed in different cultural contexts. While it is unlikely that any parent, regardless of culture, would desire that their children live the furtive life of an undocumented migrant, Engebrigtsen's perspective does question the receiving country's assumptions of the children's needs and of their particular source of distress. According to Engebrigtsen, "the general proposition that child migration leads to psychological trauma is also problematic."[8] Ensor similarly argues that "Migration, colonialism, and missionary activity served as vehicles through which white middle-class Western notions of childhood, and their associated Western academic discourses, were exported to the world in the nineteenth century."[9] She contends that it is this imposition of cultural norms that resulted in the perception of children as victimized, traumatized, and lacking agency in their own lives. On the contrary, as we will see in future chapters, undocumented university students demonstrate an admirable level of determination and strength as they not only strive for their education, but also in many cases share responsibility for the family's and community's well-being. The research presented in the following chapters indicates, from the undocumented youth's perspectives, their expressed needs and their relationships with their family members, but the research findings also illustrate that the students' own fortitude and agency are no less responsible for their positive outcomes than is the support and access they are granted. Within the U.S. context, increased sensitivity to the needs of undocumented students, which are influenced by their culture and the centrality of their relationships with their family members, will likely lead to more beneficial responses.

The dominant models of international migration, while useful in some respects, tend to emphasize the receiving country's perspective, which is in this case U.S.-centric. For instance, the dual labor market approach to international migration is based on the segmentation of the labor market and labor demands in the receiving country. Similarly, the neoclassical economics approach is largely dependent on the relative economic stability of the host country. That these models emphasize the destination country suggests an incomplete consideration of the economic disparity, political strife, and unrestrained violence that propel Mexicans, Central Americans, and others into the uncertainty and instability of migrating without legal status.

Undocumented Children

Theoretical approaches to the study of international migration tend to focus on the decision-making process that leads migrants to make the journey. Although other theories emphasize the mechanisms that perpetuate migration, the models tend to be built on the assumption that there is a rational decision-maker, who is typically the migrant. Accompanying family members are considered only marginally. Children are not expected to be part of the decision-making process, nor do they play major economic roles; they are consequently omitted from the theoretical considerations of migration. This perhaps contributes to the dearth of literature on the experiences of undocumented students. As Pérez and Cortés underscore, the limited literature that does exist on undocumented students suggests that undocumented students contend with a range of psychological concerns stemming primarily from the fear that their status will be discovered, and also from the accompanying social isolation of having to keep their personal lives secret.[10] Financial hardship represents yet another source of stress for undocumented students and their families.

Immigration and Human Capital

DebBurman argues that the proclivity for individuals to "invest in human capital in order to maximize their net wealth" is the defining characteristic of human capital theory.[11] The attainment of higher education signifies an investment in human capital that will likely result in upward socio-economic mobility, and scholars typically agree that education is one of the most effective means by which to develop human capital.[12] However, Chiswick has shown that migrants are not always able to immediately transfer their skills and education into earning potential.[13] Rather, it is the skills and education that they acquire after having migrated that seem to have the greatest positive impact on their earning potential. Similarly, studies of the children of immigrants, which tend to focus on those born in the United States, suggest that the second generation has higher levels of education, occupational aspirations, and labor market outcomes than first-generation immigrants.[14] Based on this assumption, undocumented children are more likely than their parents to see significant human capital returns on their investment in higher education, which they acquire after migration. However, even though child migrants have the potential to enjoy some of the advantages of the second generation, those who are undocumented do not share the unhindered access to educational and professional advancement. Consequently, restrictions on access to higher education for undocumented students symbolize limitations on their human capital and potential for upward socioeconomic mobility.[15]

DebBurman notes that much of the existing body of literature that discusses educational attainment among immigrants does not distinguish between different generations of immigration—that is, whether they are first, second, or third generation immigrants. She underscores the importance of making the distinction between generations, as experiences and educational attainment are likely to differ between first- and second-generation immigrants.[16] While her analysis of educational attainment by immigrant generation is a useful contribution to the literature, what is notably absent from the discussion is a consideration of the educational preparation, experiences, and attainment of the distinct population of children who, while first-generation, migrate at such a young age that they effectively grow up in the United States and are subject to its educational system. This population is often referred to as the 1.5 generation, a term that was coined by Ruben Rumbaut.[17] Similarly, other studies that do make the distinction between immigrant generations in assessing educational attainment, such as Baum and Flores's study of the experiences of children of immigrant families in higher education,[18] assume that children of immigrant families are born in the destination country rather than being immigrants themselves. Although they resemble second-generation immigrants in their levels of acculturation, the 1.5 generation, as described by Zhou, are "children who straddle the old and the new worlds but are fully part of neither."[19] As such, students of the 1.5-generation often experience a "dual frame of reference" which scholars argue allows them to "persist in the face of difficulties in the new country."[20] The students who are the focus of this study comprise this unique population, who are socialized and educated in the United States, yet their undocumented status adds an additional layer of complexity to their ability to adapt, as they lack the rights and privileges that their peers enjoy.

The assumption that undocumented children have greater potential for the development of human capital than their parents do (based on socialization in the U.S., English language acquisition, and access to education, even if it is limited to secondary education) is related to the new household economics of migration, which suggests that factors related to the human capital potential of other family members are likely to be considered in the decision to migrate. Although the parents of undocumented students appear to be generally unaware of the possibilities for their children's access to higher education, there is a general sense that even with a secondary education, both income and quality of life are improved in the destination country, perhaps based on noneconomic factors. Despite the general lack of awareness of the possibilities for undocumented students' access to higher education, their parents are aware of the greater availability of opportunities and resources in the United States than there is in the sending countries, which are primarily in Latin America. The act of migrating, then, signifies a step toward the development of human capital, if not for the parents, then at least for the children.

Networks and Social Capital

Portes and Rumbaut define social capital as "the ability to gain access to needed resources by virtue of membership in social networks and larger social structures."[21] They also argue that it is not just an individual's human capital that determines her or his pathway toward integration into the host society, but rather the broader context of the receiving society, which includes immigration and integration policies as well as social networks. The context of reception has the capacity to obstruct or facilitate integration and upward mobility among immigrants as well as the second generation.[22] Social capital is central to the process through which most undocumented students gain admission to universities. The research findings of this project underscore that the general lack of transparency and the clandestine nature of admitting undocumented students into universities is such that it is difficult—if not impossible—for even those with the greatest intellectual abilities and resourcefulness (i.e., human capital) to access these institutions without the help of their social networks of teachers, guidance counselors, clergy, and university staff. The connections that they or their family members have with others who are able to provide them with the guidance and resources to enter institutions of higher education represent their social capital, which is essential to the reduction or elimination of barriers to their educational and occupational mobility. These networks and the families and communities that build them also create a sense of belonging among immigrants.[23]

Children who immigrate, or the 1.5-generation, are distinct from both their parents and the U.S.-born children of immigrants in their experiences, immigration status, and the ways in which they integrate in the host society and develop their social capital. The 1.5-generation is able to benefit from the duality of their potential for acculturation in the United States based on their young age at arrival, and their facility with the language and culture of their home country. These characteristics offer them the dexterity to navigate both worlds. Portes and Rumbaut agree that this adroitness with the cultures of the home and host societies facilitates the development of social capital. They note that "Social capital is the factor accounting for the paradox that more successful integration to American society does not depend on complete acculturation but rather on selective preservation of immigrant parents' culture and the collective ties that go with it."[24] As immigrants (or more likely the second generation) acculturate, they may lose access to ethnic enclaves, networks, and the social capital that they provide. Bounded solidarity, a concept that refers to the tendency for ethnic or national groups to form communities based on their shared ethnic or national identity, allows members of the 1.5 or second generation to develop or maintain their relationships with their ethnic communities, keeping their networks intact.[25] The significance of social networks is further underscored by Zhou, who states:

> In our view, immigrant cultural orientations are not only rooted in the social structure of the immigrant community but also are responsive to social environment surrounding the community. In disadvantaged neighborhoods where difficult conditions and disruptive elements are often found, immigrant families may have to consciously preserve traditional values by means of ethnic solidarity to prevent the next generation from assimilating into the underprivileged segments of American society in which their community is located . . . ethnic social integration creates a form of social capital that enables an immigrant family to receive ongoing support and direction from other families and from the religious and social associations of the ethnic group . . . We thus conclude that social capital is crucial and, under certain conditions, more important than traditional human capital for the successful adaptation of younger-generation immigrants.[26]

Acculturation and Reception

As immigrants and their children adapt to their new societies, they face the risk of losing their cultural identity or the networks that facilitate their adjustment and upward socioeconomic mobility. During earlier waves of European migration to the United States immigrants generally strove to become American, and assimilation was a linear path toward an Anglo-American identity. Since the shift in immigrant source countries and regions that occurred in the mid-twentieth century, considerations of acculturation and assimilation have become more nuanced in order to represent the increased diversity of the immigrant populations. Several models have emerged to indicate that adapting to a new society does not necessarily mean assimilation in the sense that it did during earlier waves of migration. Portes and Rumbaut (2014) distinguish acculturation from assimilation by defining the former as the first step in the process toward adapting to a new society, and the latter as the final stage of this process. Segmented assimilation has emerged as a concept that delineates the different options that immigrants have in their paths to acculturation: upward assimilation toward the middle class, downward assimilation toward the underclass, or upward educational and economic mobility while preserving cultural identity. Although an analysis of the ways in which undocumented students acculturate in the United States was beyond the scope of this project, their presence in institutions of higher education, combined with their expressed commitment to their families and communities, suggest that they embrace the latter form of integration, which enables them to preserve their social capital within their ethnic communities while simultaneously establishing networks within the U.S. mainstream.

As a result, students must navigate their identity as undocumented in a transitional phase in their life course, from being legally protected as minors in educational systems, to that of adults whose citizenship status is suddenly their responsibility once they turn 18. This is also occurring in the context of selective colleges that are not generally sites of racial diversity and may differ significantly from the neighborhoods and high schools from which students came. As such, students are also encountering aspects of their identities they may have never considered before including being a member of a racial minority group as well as having a social class background not widely represented in most private colleges and universities. The larger societal context becomes more apparent to students in this phase of their lives, in particular the larger realities of racial oppression that persists in the U.S. context.[27]

The Role of Institutions

Institutions, in their various forms, sizes, and capacities, both formal and informal, play a role in the processes of migration and integration, and in the development of social capital among immigrants. While institutions can be conceptualized as a set of rules or norms that govern behavior,[28] the consideration here includes a plethora of institutions that interface with immigrants, from governmental institutions to immigrant organizations, churches, and schools, the latter being of particular interest. According to Diaz-Strong et al.:

> Institutions of higher education play a key role in helping students locate resources necessary to achieve their educational goals. While supporting, advocating, and waiting for legislation that provides a pathway for all undocumented persons, institutions can take steps to

assist students in the present. Institutions must be transparent and purposefully communicate institutional policies and available resources to faculty, staff, and feeder high schools. In addition, institutions must partner internally and externally to increase private and institutional financial resources for undocumented students. Having one or two scholarships available or providing a list of online websites is simply not enough to meet the need. Finally, community colleges and universities must partner and create programs to help undocumented students make a seamless transition and locate resources that help them complete their education.[29]

Diaz-Strong et al. underscore the role of educational institutions in facilitating undocumented students' access to universities. Still, accommodating undocumented students in universities can be mutually beneficial to the students and the institutions. The majority of universities in the United States have in their mission statements or strategic goals messages that tout their diversity (often indicating the school's racial or ethnic diversity among the other credentials and demographic indicators) or that indicate their recognition of the benefits of diverse student and faculty bodies. Institutions actively seek to recruit and retain students and faculty whose racial, ethnic, or gender identities, among other forms of identity, contribute to the richness that is characteristic of a diverse academic environment. Undocumented students represent another layer of diversity in the experiences that they have encountered and the perspectives that they can add to academic discourses, and institutions can consider it an honor that they are able to attract such students, whose enrollment and matriculation likely involved greater effort than is typical.

As DebBurman remarks, education is central to the development of human capital, and educational institutions share the responsibility for fostering human capital among immigrants and ethnic minorities:

> long-term structural changes in the U.S. economy have markedly increased the importance of education, making postsecondary education a minimum requirement for any individual to compete successfully in the labor market. Thus, educational institutions in the U.S. today are faced with a two-fold issue: one, to educate a larger and more diverse population and, two, to bridge the gap in educational attainment among the various ethnic groups.[30]

Conclusion

Undocumented students—or undocumented youth more generally—may not necessarily fit the parameters that these models of international migration suggest, given that most of them arrived as children when the decision was not theirs. However, these models serve as explanatory tools to improve the understanding of the circumstances that motivate parents to migrate with children but without the legal status that would afford them the opportunity to live full, free lives without fear of deportation and with access to education, employment, and other basic privileges such as driving and traveling. There is no question that the choice to migrate under these circumstances can be dangerous, and even after the migration process is complete life as an undocumented immigrant severely restricts one's opportunities. The various models of international migration discussed here underscore that despite the difficulties of the life as an undocumented immigrant, which is usually not a mystery to prospective immigrants, the circumstances in the sending country are such that even a life with limited educational or employment opportunities surpasses life in the challenging context of the home country. From the perspective of the "push-pull" model, the push factors are so consequential that even the difficulties of a life without legal status and the constant threat of deportation are not enough to deter immigration. The pull factors, or the opportunities that accompany a life that is hopeful in contrast—even for those without legal immigration status—make immigration to the United States the more attractive option.

Notes

1. Ravenstein, "Laws of Migration," 167–235.

2. E. S. Lee, "Theory of Migration," 47–57.

3. United Nations Office on Drugs and Crime, *Global Study on Homicide 2013: Trends, Contexts*, Data, accessed July 13, 2015, http://www.unodc.org/documents/gsh/pdfs/2014_GLOBAL_HOMICIDE_BOOK_web.pdf.

4. Douglas S. Massey, Jorge Durand, and Nolan J. Malone, *Beyond Smoke and Mirrors: Mexican Immigration in an Era of Economic Integration* (New York: Russell Sage Foundation, 2002). Tanya Golash-Boza, *Immigration Nation: Raids, Detentions, and Deportations in Post-9/11 America* (London: Paradigm Publishers, 2012).

5. Jones, *Jamaican Immigrants*.

6. Porumbescu, "Migration Policies," 165–175.

7. Engebrigtsen, "The Child's—or the State's—Best Interests?," 191–200.

8. Ibid., 196.

9. Ensor, "Understanding Migrant Children: Conceptualizations, Approaches, and Issues," in *Children and Migration: At the Crossroads of Resiliency and Vulnerability*, ed. Marisa O. Ensor and Elzbieta M. Gozdziak (Basingstoke: Palgrave Macmillan, 2010), 17.

10. Pérez and Cortés, *Undocumented Latino College Students*.

11. DebBurman, *Immigrant Education*, 21.

12. Duleep and Regets, "Immigrants and Human-Capital Investment," 186–191. See also Friedberg, "Immigrant Assimilation and the Portability of Human Capital," 221–251; and Sharaf, "Earnings of Immigrants," 1–18.

13. Chiswick, "Earnings of Foreign-Born Men," 897–921. See also Chiswick and Miller, "Why Is the Payoff to Schooling Smaller for Immigrants?," 1317–1340.

14. Portes and Rumbaut, *Legacies*. See also Portes and Rumbaut, *Ethnicities*; and DebBurman, *Immigrant Education*.

15. Diaz-Strong et al., "Purged," 107–119.

16. DebBurman, *Immigrant Education*.

17. Min Zhou, "Growing Up American," 63–95.

18. Baum and Flores, "Children in Immigrant Families," 171–193.

19. Zhou, "Growing Up American," 65.

20. S. J. Lee, *Up Against Whiteness*, 54.

21. Portes and Rumbaut, "Forging of a New America," 313.

22. Portes and Rumbaut, "Forging of a New America"; Jones, *Jamaican Immigrants*.

23. O'Neill, *Asylum, Migration, and Community*.

24. Portes and Rumbaut, "Forging of a New America," 313.

25. Portes and Sensenbrenner, "Embeddedness and Immigration," 1320–1350.

26. Zhou and Bankston, "Social Capital," 821.

27. Blauner, *Racial Oppression in America*.

28. Coyne and Boettke, "Institutions, Immigration, and Identity."

29. Diaz-Strong et al., "Purged," 117.

30. DebBurman, *Immigrant Education*, 1.

References

Baum, Sandy, and Stella M. Flores. "Higher Education and Children in Immigrant Families." *The Future of Children* 21, no. 1 (2011): 171–193.

Blauner, Robert. *Racial Oppression in America*. New York: Harper & Row, 1972.

Bloch, Alice, Nando Sigona, and Roger Zetter. *Sans Papiers: The Social and Economic Lives of Young Undocumented Migrants*. London: Pluto Press, 2014.

Chiswick, Barry R. "The Effect of Americanization on the Earnings of Foreign-Born Men." *Journal of Political Economy* 86, no. 5 (Oct. 1978): 897–921.

Chiswick, Barry R., and Paul W. Miller. "Why Is the Payoff to Schooling Smaller for Immigrants?" *Labour Economics* 15, no. 6 (2008): 1317–1340.

Coyne, Christopher J., and Peter J. Boettke. "Institutions, Immigration, and Identity." *NYU Journal of Law & Liberty* 2, no. 131 (2006).

DebBurman, Noyna. *Immigrant Education: Variations by Generation, Age-at-Immigration, and Country of Origin*. New York: LFB Scholarly, 2005.

Diaz-Strong, Daysi, Christina Gómez, Maria E. Luna-Duarte, and Erica R. Meiners. "Purged: Undocumented Students, Financial Aid Policies, and Access to Higher Education." *Journal of Hispanic Higher Education* 10, no. 2 (2011): 107–119.

Duleep, Harriet Orcutt, and Mark C. Regets. "Immigrants and Human-Capital Investment." *The American Economic Review* 89, no. 2 (1999): 186–191.

Duncan, Brian, and Stephen J. Trejo. "Assessing the Socioeconomic Mobility and Integration of U.S. Immigrants and Their Descendants." *The Annals of the American Academy of Political and Social Science* 657, no. 1 (2015): 108–135.

Engebrigtsen, Ada. "The Child's—or the State's—Best Interests? An Examination of the Ways Immigration Officials Work with Unaccompanied Asylum Seeking Minors in Norway." *Child and Family Social Work* 8, no. 3 (2003): 191–200.

Ensor, Marisa O., and Elzbieta M. Gozdziak. *Children and Migration: At the Crossroads of Resiliency and Vulnerability*. Basingstoke: Palgrave Macmillan, 2010.

Friedberg, Rachel M. "You Can't Take It with You?: Immigrant Assimilation and the Portability of Human Capital." *Journal of Labor Economics* 18, no. 2 (2000): 221–251.

Hagan, Jacqueline Maria. *Migration Miracle: Faith, Hope, and Meaning on the Undocumented Journey*. Cambridge, Mass.: Harvard University Press, 2008.

Jones, Terry-Ann. *Jamaican Immigrants in the United States and Canada: Race, Transnationalism, and Social Capital*. New York: LFB Scholarly, 2008.

Lee, Everett S. "A Theory of Migration." *Demography* 3, no. 1 (1966): 47–57.

Lee, Stacey J. *Up Against Whiteness: Race, School, and Immigrant Youth*. New York: Teachers College Press, 2005.

Lopez, Janet K. *Undocumented Students and the Policies of Wasted Potential*. El Paso, Tex.: LFB Scholarly Publishing, 2010.

Nair-Reichert, Usha, and Richard J. Cebula. "Access to Higher Public Education and Location Choices of Undocumented Migrants: An Exploratory

Analysis." *International Advances in Economic Research* 21, no. 2 (2015): 189–199.

Olivas, Michael A. *No Undocumented Child Left Behind: Plyler v. Doe and the Education of Undocumented Schoolchildren.* New York University Press, 2012.

O'Neill, Maggie. *Asylum, Migration, and Community.* Bristol: Policy Press, 2010.

Pan, Ying. "The Impact of Legal Status on Immigrants' Earnings and Human Capital: Evidence from the IRCA 1986." *Journal of Labor Research* 33, no. 2 (2012): 119–142.

Paraskevopoulou, Anna. "Undocumented Worker Transitions: Family Migration." *International Journal of Sociology and Social Policy* 31, no. 1, 2 (2011): 110–122.

Pérez, William. *We are Americans: Undocumented Students Pursuing the American Dream.* Sterling, Va.: Stylus, 2009.

Pérez, William, and Richard Douglas Cortés. *Undocumented Latino College Students: Their Socioemotional and Academic Experiences.* El Paso, Tex.: LFB Scholarly Publishing, 2011.

Portes, Alejandro, and Rubén G. Rumbaut. "Conclusion: The Forging of a New America: Lessons for Theory and Policy." In *Ethnicities: Children of Immigrants in America*, edited by Rubén G. Rumbaut and Alejandro Portes. New York; Berkeley: University of California Press, 2001.

———. *Immigrant America: A Portrait.* 4th ed. Berkeley: University of California Press, 2014.

———. *Legacies: The Story of the Immigrant Second Generation.* New York; Berkeley: University of California Press, 2001.

Portes, Alejandro, and Julia Sensenbrenner. "Embeddedness and Immigration: Notes on the Social Determinants of Economic Action." *The American Journal of Sociology* 98, no. 6 (May 1993): 1320–1350.

Porumbescu, Alexandra. "Migration Policies in the European Union: Espoused Perspectives and Practices-in-Use." *Revista de Stiinte Politice* 4, no. 46 (2015): 165–175.

Ravenstein, E. G. "The Laws of Migration." *Journal of the Statistical Society of London* 48, no. 2 (June 1885): 167–235.

Rincón, Alejandra. *Undocumented Immigrants and Higher Education: Sí se Puede!* New York: LFB Scholarly Publishing, 2008.

Rumbaut, Rubén G., and Alejandro Portes, eds. *Ethnicities: Children of Immigrants in America.* New York; Berkeley: University of California Press, 2001.

Sassen, Saskia. *Expulsions: Brutality and Complexity in the Global Economy.* Cambridge, Mass.: The Belknap Press of Harvard University Press, 2014.

Sharaf, Mesbah Fathy. "The Earnings of Immigrants and the Quality Adjustment of Immigrant Human Capital." *IZA Journal of Migration* 2, no. 1 (2013): 1–18.

United Nations Office on Drugs and Crime. *Global Study on Homicide 2013: Trends, Contexts.* Data, accessed July 13, 2015, http://www.unodc.org /documents/gsh/pdfs/2014_GLOBAL_HOMICIDE_BOOK_web.pdf.

Zhou, Min. "Growing Up American: The Challenge Confronting Immigrant Children and Children of Immigrants." *Annual Review of Sociology* 23, no. 1 (1997): 63–95.

Zhou, Min, and Carl L. Bankston III. "Social Capital and the Adaptation of the Second Generation: The Case of Vietnamese Youth in New Orleans." *The International Migration Review* 28, no. 4 (1994): 821–845.

2   Immigration, Jesuit Higher Education, and the Undocumented

KURT SCHLICHTING

Immigration and the American Experience

Long before the American Revolution and the adoption of the Constitution in 1789, immigration shaped the American experience. Spanish explorers traveled north from Mexico into the future state of Arizona in 1539 and European settlement followed along the eastern seaboard: Jamestown, Virginia, 1607, and Plymouth, Massachusetts, 1620.

From 1819, when the United States government began to systematically collect immigration data through the year 2014, the official number of immigrants totals 79,483,571. Almost 80 million people came to the United States in 195 years, the most massive movement of population to one place in all of recorded history. As Oscar Handlin, the renowned historian, argued, in opposition to Fredrick Jackson Turner's frontier thesis, the history that decisively shaped the United States is the history of immigration and not the settling of the West.[1] The history of the United States is the history of immigration.

Almost all Americans have a story of immigration at the heart of their family's narrative history. At Thanksgiving or a graduation a respected elder may tell the story, typically in epic terms, beginning with the challenging journey across the ocean to the new world. It may involve a beloved grandfather and grandmother or a much earlier time in American history. Details are vague, as the details do not matter. What matters is the arc of the story: hardship, struggle, hard work, and then triumph. Failure and disappointment are edited out. In our current polarized political climate, many of the harshest critics of immigration have conveniently forgotten their own family's immigration story.

For the first 150 years of the country's history, regulation of immigration remained minimal. There was no inspection process on the docks of

New York or Boston, no documents to present. In the nineteenth century, there were no "undocumented" immigrants for the simple reason that no documents were required. In 1819 the federal government began to collect immigration data by requiring all ships arriving to prepare a "manifest" listing arriving passengers for the Collector of Customs in U.S. ports.[2] There were no federal or state immigration officials. Not until 1924 did federal law require an immigrant visa obtained from a U.S. embassy for entry to America.

The founding of the Jesuit universities follows the history of immigration. The first Jesuit university, Georgetown, was founded in 1789 by John Carroll, who in 1808 was appointed the Archbishop of Baltimore. Maryland was the one American colony with a significant Catholic population. In the nineteenth century, twenty-one Jesuit universities were established, most in the country's burgeoning cities—Boston, New York, St. Louis, Seattle, San Francisco—filled with immigrants, primarily from Europe. The Jesuits' mission was clear: to provide an opportunity for Catholic immigrants and their children to have access to a college education and to reach for the American dream of upward mobility. As the twenty-first century begins, Jesuit higher education remains committed to providing that opportunity, including students from families who have recently arrived—just as the Catholic immigrants did over two hundred years ago.

Throughout American history immigrants have arrived in "waves," leaving their homelands and undertaking the arduous journey to the promised land. In the eighteenth and nineteenth centuries the journey involved a long voyage across the oceans in frail wooden ships, navigated by the sun and stars. Today the voyage may be by foot through the Americas or on a crowded jet airplane, but the challenge remains: to venture and then adjust to a new life in a new world. And the origins of the people coming to the United States have changed over time. In the nineteenth century the vast numbers of immigrants left from Europe; today a small number of immigrants arrive from Europe by comparison. The majority now arrive from Asia and Central America. Wherever people have journeyed from, they share a common desire: to have a decent life, to practice their religious faith, to give their children and their children's children the opportunity to use their imagination, energy, and talent for themselves and their American society.

Colonial America

In the early colonies, the British dominated the settlement of the eastern seaboard and established both formal and informal rules governing who could settle in their territories. Susan Martin, in *A Nation of Immigrants*,[3] provides three different models the colonies evolved to deal with new migrants to America: the Virginia, Massachusetts, and Pennsylvania models. Significant differences prevailed:

Virginia Model:
Small number of early settlers—fortune seekers—an insatiable
    demand for labor
Immigrants valued for their labor recruited/transported to colony
    but rights restricted
        indentured servants
        convicts
        slaves

Massachusetts Model:
Settled by Puritans to establish a religious community—sought
    freedom to pursue *their* religious beliefs
        Immigrants who shared religious beliefs welcomed
        Newcomers who did not share religious beliefs/values faced
            set of restrictions and exclusionary practices

Pennsylvania Model:
Open to people of different faiths—actively encouraged
    immigration. Challenge—to integrate immigrants into a
    pluralistic society
        Rules for immigrants: foreign settlers required to register and
            all ships arriving required to maintain list of non-British
            immigrants
        Rules for "naturalization" of non-British immigrants
        Ethnic and religious pluralism with concerns about ability
            and willingness of immigrants to integrate and
            assimilate

Over time, the Pennsylvania Model shaped the American immigration experience. During the "Century of Immigration," 1820–1920, people could come to the United States with few restrictions, the Chinese being the exception, until the immigration restriction laws in 1924 closed the "Golden Door." The concerns raised about immigrants in the Pennsylvania colony, the road to citizenship, and the question of assimilation persist till today.

The New Republic

Questions about immigration remained after the American Revolution and the adoption of the Constitution in 1793. Thomas Jefferson's concerns, given the small number of immigrants, focused on the time he estimated it would take to settle the territory of the country, especially after the Louisiana Purchase in 1803. In 1804 he predicted that the settlement of American territory, beyond the Appalachian Mountains, would take one thousand years. Jefferson assumed a low level of immigration for the foreseeable future and could not envision the waves of people from all over the world who would journey to the U.S. in the nineteenth century.

Regulation of immigration at the federal or state level remained minimal. Article 1, Section 7 of the Constitution required the federal government "to establish a uniform Rule of Naturalization," the process for becoming a citizen; the Constitution *did not* set out any legal parameters for the federal government to regulate immigration, the process of "coming to America." Implicitly the framers expected that immigration would continue, as it had in the eighteenth century; the federal government's power would be to regulate "naturalization" and *not to regulate* or control immigration.

Controversy then surrounded naturalization as it does immigration today; in 1790 Congress mandated that "free white persons" could become citizens after two years, in 1795 the time requirement was extended to five years, in 1798 to fourteen years, and in 1802 back to five years, which remained the law for over one hundred years and set the stage for the "Century of Immigration."

The Century of Immigration—First Phase 1820–1865

At the dawn of the nineteenth century immigration to the United States was limited; the War of 1812 (1812–1815) devastated American commerce and transatlantic shipping dramatically declined, limiting the movement of immigrants from Europe. After the War of 1812 immigration resumed on a modest scale but in the early 1820s, and continuing for over one hundred years, a veritable flood of people crossed the Atlantic (and the Pacific) and arrived in the American port cities setting off the Century of Immigration. A nation with a population of 9,638,453, including 1,538,022 slaves, grew to 106,021,537 people in 1920—from just under 10 to over 106 million in a century! Over 35 million immigrants came to the United States and changed the course of American history.

In the first half of the century most of the immigrants came from northern Europe, Britain, Ireland, and Germany; push-pull factors created massive immigration flows. While America represented the "Golden Door" to a better life, the Irish Potato Famine forced over 1.4 million Irish to leave Ireland.[4] Agricultural and industrial unrest in Germany led to mass migration to the United States; population growth and limited agricultural land forced many to leave Norway and Sweden.

Overwhelmingly immigrants settled in the American cities, first in the port cities of Boston, Baltimore, Philadelphia, and of course New York, which served as the primary entry port. Many were Catholic and the Jesuits responded by opening universities: Boston—Boston College in 1863, Baltimore—Loyola University in 1852, Philadelphia—St. Joseph's University in 1851, and New York—Fordham University in 1841.

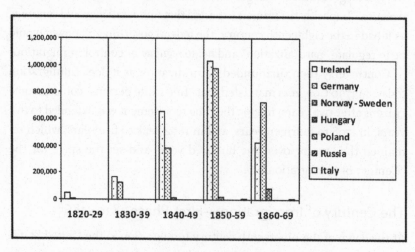

FIGURE 2-1. Century of Immigration 1820–1869: Country of Origin. (Source: U.S. Department of Homeland Security, *Yearbook of Immigration Statistics*, 2012.)

Boston College's website's "History" page clearly ties the founding of the university to the Irish immigrant population in South Boston:

FROM THE SOUTH END TO CHESTNUT HILL

Boston College was founded by the Society of Jesus in 1863 and, with three teachers and 22 students, opened its doors on September 5, 1864. Through its first seven decades, it remained a small undergraduate institution, offering the sons of the Irish working class a rigorous course load in theology and philosophy, classical languages, rhetoric, math and science.[5]

The reference from the "South End" to "Chestnut Hill" describes the relocation of the campus from the Irish South End to the upper-middle-class Boston suburb of Chestnut Hill in the early nineteenth century. It also reflects the rise of an immigrant population from poverty to affluence; a history in which Boston College played a central role. Fordham University, originally St. John's University, celebrates a similar founding story:

The origins of Fordham University can be traced to 1839 when John Hughes, the Bishop of New York, bought 100 acres at Rose Hill in the Fordham section of what was then Westchester County . . . . The financial difficulties that John Hughes faced in starting St. John's College [Fordham] are indicative of the poverty of the New York Catholic community in 1841. It took a brave man to start a college under such circumstances, but Hughes, an Irish immigrant himself, saw education as the *indispensable means* for his immigrant flock to break out of the cycle of poverty and better themselves economically and socially in their adopted homeland.[6]

Other Catholic immigrants traveled to the Midwest from New York via the Erie Canal and the Great Lakes to where their labor was welcomed: steel mills in Cleveland, slaughter houses in Cincinnati and Chicago, and the building of the Transcontinental Railroad from Omaha to San Francisco after the Civil War. Gangs of Irish laborers built the Union Pacific Railroad constructing the railroad west from Omaha. Irish immigrants and their families settled in Omaha and Creighton University opened in 1878. On the west coast, the Catholic immigrants moved to San Francisco, San Jose, Seattle and Spokane, Washington, and the Jesuits followed: Santa

Clara University in 1851, University of San Francisco in 1888, University of Seattle in 1891, and Gonzaga University in 1881 in Spokane.

The arrival of tens of thousands of Catholic immigrants created tension; the memory of the Protestant Reformation and the century of bloody religious warfare that traumatized Europe remained vivid. Anti-Catholicism arose and grew more virulent as the number of Catholic immigrants increased. For the Famine Irish, the anti-Catholicism they encountered was coupled with the centuries-old ethnic and political conflict over British rule, which continued in the United States where the first immigrants were from British Isles.[7] John Higham, in his seminal work, *Strangers in the Land: Patterns of Nativism 1860–1825*,[8] characterized anti-Catholicism as "the most luxuriant, tenacious tradition of paranoiac agitation in American history."

Anti-Catholic riots occurred in 1834 in Boston, where a mob burned the Ursuline Covent school; in 1844 in Philadelphia a Protestant-led mob burned St. Augustine's Church. In addition to physical violence, Catholic immigrants encountered legal barriers to assimilation. For example, Connecticut did not disestablish the Congregational Church until 1820, and decades later, with the first attempt to build a Catholic church in Fairfield, Connecticut, vocal opposition and threats of legal action followed. Rhode Island, proud of its history of religious tolerance, did not eliminate property qualifications for voting until after the Dorr Rebellion in 1844 and continued property qualifications for immigrant males until 1888. The property qualification was explicitly directed at the Irish immigrants.

Newspapers and popular magazines in the nineteenth century were filled with anti-immigrant editorials, stories of the drunkenness of the Irish and the German Catholics for frequenting their beer gardens on the Sabbath. Thomas Nast, the famous cartoonist justly celebrated for his political cartoons which attacked the corrupt Tammany Hall political machine, also used the cartoon to cast aspersions on the Irish and the rise of the Catholic Church in America. Nast systematically depicted the Irish as drunks, politically corrupt, violent, and a threat to American values. Nast also depicted the Irish as apes and implicitly as non-white.

Nast and others questioned whether the Irish and other Catholics could ever be assimilated, the key question raised by the Pennsylvania Model, and the battle lines emerged over the question of public versus Catholic education. Political and legal battles over education raged across the coun-

FIGURE 2-2. Thomas Nast—*Harpers Weekly*, September 30, 1871.

try and reached the Supreme Court. Catholics feared the influence of the Protestants over public education and withdrew and set out, at great expense, to build a parallel system of primary and secondary schools and universities of which the Jesuit universities are a part. Nast was not content to simply let the Catholics proceed on their own; he viewed the Catholic Church and its clergy as threats to public education. In a famous Harper's cartoon in 1871, he depicted the Catholic bishops as crocodiles set to devour American children while the corrupt leaders of Tammany Hall, led by Boss Tweed, approve in the background (Figure 2-2).

Anti-Catholicism continued for the rest of the Century of Immigration and fueled the growth of Nativism, the Know Nothing Party, and widespread political pressure to limit immigration. Even as Irish immigration declined after the Civil War, Catholics from Poland, Hungary, and Italy arrived in huge numbers and encountered the same prejudice and suspicion as the Irish. By the time of the arrival of large numbers of Catholic immigrants from eastern Europe and Italy, Catholic schools in cities across the U.S. would offer a primary and secondary education and the Jesuit, and other Catholic universities, would provide opportunity for a college education.

After the Civil War, immigration resumed and in fact increased dramatically over the next fifty years, especially in the first two decades of

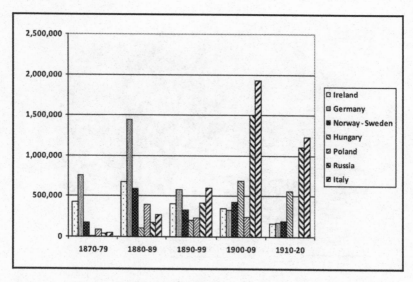

FIGURE 2-3. Century of Immigration 1870–1920: Country of Origin. (Source: U.S. Department of Homeland Security, *Yearbook of Immigration Statistics, 2012.*)

the twentieth century (Figure 2-3). Between 1900 and 1909, over 8 million immigrants arrived (8,202,000), including 1.9 million from Italy and 1.5 million from Russia, almost all Jewish. In the next twenty years immigration totaled 6.4 million, with an additional 1.2 million from Italy and 1.1 million from Russia.

As with earlier waves of European immigrants, the majority found their way to the industrial cities on the East Coast, Midwest, and Far West where they provided the labor to fuel the American industrial revolution and what the historian Howard Mumford Jones labeled the "Age of Energy."[9] In the fifty years after the end of the Civil War until the outbreak of WWI in 1914 the United States became the leading economic power in the world.

Again the Jesuits followed, opening eight more universities: Milwaukee— Marquette, 1861; Buffalo—Canisus, 1870; Chicago—Loyola, 1870; Jersey City—St. Peter's, 1872; Denver—Regis, 1877; Omaha—Creighton, 1878; Spokane—Gonzaga, 1881; and Cleveland—John Carroll, 1886. All of these "new" universities remained dedicated to serving the immigrants and their children. Other Catholic religious orders followed the lead of the Jesuits, opening universities to serve a growing Catholic population.

Immigration Regulation

In the past few decades the United States has been engaged in a bitter political debate and a cultural war over immigration. Who can come to America, under what conditions, and what is the road to citizenship? If people have arrived who are "undocumented," can they remain? How aggressively should the federal government pursue those who are undocumented and return them to their country of origin? Those questions echo concerns raised during the Century of Immigration. However, they more strongly reflect the political and cultural divide that erupted at the dawn of the twentieth century than at the beginning of the nineteenth century.

Immigration regulation was almost nonexistent in the first half of the nineteenth century. Immigrant ships arrived in port cities such as New York, and the only regulatory process was for an officer to proceed to the Customs House with a ship's manifest listing all passengers and their country of origin. For the newly arrived immigrants, there was no requirement that they have any official documents to enter; they simply walked down the gangplank and set foot in the promised land. However the waterfront was not a safe place. The docking of an immigrant ship created a chaotic scene. All sorts of shady characters haunted the docks and preyed upon the newly arrived: money changers cheated on exchange rates; runners competed to drag luggage to a nearby boarding house, which overcharged for filthy accommodations and rotten food; fake agents sold bogus railroad tickets. Criminal gangs operated out of the bars and grog shops on South Street in lower Manhattan along the East River. Prostitution and gambling lured many to destitution.

Calls for reform and efforts to protect the vulnerable prompted New York State, in 1855, to establish the first immigrant arrival station in the country, Castle Garden, on the Battery in lower Manhattan, and required all immigrants to pass through the Emigrant Landing Depot. An explicit purpose of the State's initiative was to provide an orderly process to protect immigrants and not to restrict immigration. The Golden Door remained open. In the first fifteen years of operation over 2 million immigrants passed through Castle Garden, far more than any other entry port in the country (Table 2-1). New York State stands as an exemplar of the Pennsylvania Model.

Table 2-1. Immigrants Processed at
Castle Garden in New York: 1855–1869

Year	Number of Immigrants
1855	136,233
1856	142,342
1857	183,773
1858	78,589
1859	79,322
1860	105,169
1861	65,589
1862	76,306
1863	156,844
1864	182,296
1865	196,352
1866	238,418
1867	242,731
1868	213,686
1869	258,989
Total	**2,356,639**

In the second half of the Century of Immigration the flood of people coming to the United States continued. The federal government remained apart from immigration regulation with one notable exception—the Chinese. In California the Gold Rush lured tens of thousands of migrants from the East and immigrants from around the world, including those from China. The arrival of large numbers of Chinese led to a wave of anti-Chinese agitation and outright racism. They were first barred from mining and had to work as low-wage laborers during the Gold Rush. In 1862 the state of California passed the Anti-Coolie Act, which required the Chinese to acquire a state license and pay a tax to work in the mines or open a business; no other immigrants faced this restriction.

Efforts to exclude the Chinese continued until the United States Congress passed the Chinese Exclusion Act in 1882 prohibiting all immigration of Chinese laborers and made the naturalization process for Chinese already here much more difficult. The Chinese in the United States were classified as "permanent aliens" and could never become citizens. The Exclusion Act was the first time in American history that people from a specific country of origin were denied entry. The anti-Chinese efforts in California represented rising anti-immigrant sentiment in the United States, which would expand and sharpen over the coming decades and lead to drastic immigration restriction in the early twentieth century.

With the flood of immigrants continuing, vocal anti-immigration forces demanded that the federal government exclude other "undesirable" immigrants along with the Chinese: prostitutes and convicts (1875), impoverished immigrants likely to become a burden on local government (1882), and laborers under contract (1885). Both opponents and supporters of immigration also argued that the federal government should assume control over immigration processing, and Ellis Island opened in New York Harbor on January 2, 1892; New York State subsequently closed Castle Garden. Ellis Island would represent, metaphorically, the "Golden Door" for generations of immigrants coming to the United States in the later part of the nineteenth century and the beginning of the twentieth. An indelible image remains the arrival of groups of immigrants on Ellis Island, waiting, with their meager belongings, to begin the process of entering America. A number gaze across the harbor at the Statue of Liberty.

Closing the Golden Door

In the decade after the Civil War, 1870–1879, immigration exceeded over two and three-quarter million arrivals (2,742,137) and then doubled to over five and one-quarter million between 1880 and 1889 (5,248,568).[10] A significant shift occurred; many more immigrants now arrived from eastern and southern Europe, adding to the diversity of American society. In the decade before the turn of the century, total immigration declined; an economic panic in 1893 gave way to a full depression which lasted the next three or four years, reducing the economic incentive of immigration. Despite the recession, the number of immigrants arriving from five eastern and southern European countries exceeded the number from Ireland, Germany, Norway, and Sweden (see Table 2-2). After the turn of the century, European immigrants came in huge numbers from southern and eastern Europe and not from Ireland, Germany, or the Scandinavian countries (Table 2-3). Between 1910 and 1919 more people came from Greece than from either Ireland or Germany.

Table 2-2. Country of Origin: 1870–1879, 1880–1889, and 1890–1899

	1870–1879	1880–1889	1890–1899
Total	2,742,137	5,248,568	3,694,294
Europe	2,252,050	4,638,684	3,576,411
Northern European Countries			
Ireland	422,264	674,061	405,710
Germany	751,769	1,445,181	579,072
Norway	88,644	185,111	96,810
Sweden	90,179	401,330	237,248
Sub-total	1,352,856	2,705,683	1,318,840
Southern and Eastern European Countries			
Hungary	5,598	109,982	203,350
Poland	11,016	42,910	107,793
Russia	34,977	173,081	413,382
Italy	46,296	267,660	603,761
Greece	209	1,807	12,732
Sub-total	98,096	595,440	1,341,018

Many immigrants from southern and eastern Europe were Catholics while those arriving from Russia were Jewish. The new Catholic immigrants encountered the same anti-Catholicism that the Irish faced and the eastern European Jews faced vicious anti-Semitism.[11]

As immigration continued into the first two decades of the new century, a literal tidal wave of people came to America. In just these two decades 14.6 million immigrants arrived, including almost 2 million from Italy between 1900 and 1909! Immigrant neighborhoods in all of the major cities in the country were filled with overcrowded tenements, where people lived with little sanitation and often without access to clean water. Appalling conditions touched the conscience of progressives who increasingly advocated for reform efforts to improve the lives of the immigrants. Jacob Riis, the crusading photo-journalist, in 1890 published *How the Other Half Lives: Studies among the Tenements of New York*, and his pictures of hellish life in the Lower East Side shocked New York and people around the country.[12]

Table 2-3. Country of Origin: 1900–1909 and 1910–1919

	1900–1909	1910–1919
Total	8,202,388	6,347,380
Europe	7,572,569	4,985,411
Northern European Countries		
Ireland	344,940	166,455
Germany	328,722	174,227
Norway	182,542	79,488
Sweden	244,439	112,957
Sub-total	1,100,643	533,127
Southern and Eastern European Countries		
Hungary	685,567	565,553
Poland	n.a.ᵃ	n.a.
Russia	1,501,301	1,106,998
Italy	1,930,475	1, 229,916
Greece	145,402	198,108
Sub-total	4,262,745	3,100,575

a. Poland included in Austria, Germany, Hungary, and Russia from 1899 to 1919.

The Catholic dioceses in the American cities continued to open parochial schools, build hospitals, and support the heroic efforts of various religious orders, nuns, priests, and brothers who dedicated their lives to helping poor immigrants. Hennessey's study of Catholic communities reported a total of 2,246 parochial elementary schools, with 405,234 students in the U.S. in 1880; by 1910 the number of parochial elementary schools reached 4,845 and 1,237,251 students.[13]

While the progressive reform efforts sought to alleviate the worst of the conditions in the slums, anti-immigration forces continued to gain momentum. Three Harvard graduates formed the Immigration Restriction League in 1894, which attracted scholars and prominent supporters who began to lobby Congress. Senator Henry Cabot Lodge of Massachusetts was a vocal supporter of the League and, in 1909, called for placing restrictions on the number of people who should be allowed to enter. The League argued that the "new" immigrants, especially those from southern and eastern Europe, were racially inferior. Support for limiting immigration grew with the publication of the eugenicist Madison Grant's *The Passing of the Great Race* (1921).[14] Eugenicists purported that "scientific" research proved races/ethnicities could be "ranked" and people from southern and eastern Europe were inferior intellectually to those from the Anglo-Saxon and Nordic countries in northern Europe.

Revolutionary ferment in Europe led to Congress in 1903 banning anarchists and anyone who advocated the overthrow of the U.S. government; the Bolshevik Revolution in Russia in 1917 fanned the Red Scare in the United States and a deep suspicion of radical intellectual immigrants. The Ku Klux Klan's revival in 1915 added hatred of Catholics, Jews, and immigrants to their vicious racism and strengthened Southern political opposition to immigration. A recession followed the end of World War I, and loud voices contended that the new immigrants took jobs away from American citizens, adding an economic argument to the calls for immigration restriction.

Despite all of the anti-immigration agitation, the flood of people arriving continued in the first two decades of the twentieth century: 8.2 million entered between 1900 and 1909, and an additional 6.4 million came in the next decade. The huge numbers of immigrants arriving each year only intensified the effort of the anti-immigration forces, however, and political pressure reached a boiling point in the early 1920s; Congress finally acted.

Immigration Restriction

The Immigration Act of 1924 (Johnson-Reed Act) represented a decisive break in American history. From the adoption of the Constitution in 1787, the Pennsylvania Model of immigration had prevailed: Immigration was encouraged and few restrictions placed on who could come to America. With the Immigration Act of 1924, open immigration ended and the country moved to the Massachusetts Model, placing severe restrictions on immigration. Quotas were established and all immigrants were required to have an immigration visa issued at an American embassy. Without proper "documents," no one could enter through the Golden Door.

First the law mandated that a total of 165,000 immigrants would be admitted each year. The number of immigrants who could enter from each country was set at 2 percent of the number of people born in that country in the United Sates as enumerated in the 1890 Census. By using 1890

Census data, the clear intention of the act was to dramatically curtail immigration from southern and eastern Europe, which did not get underway, to any large extent, until after 1890. Senator Ellison DuRant Smith of South Carolina presented the eugenics argument for discriminating against the "inferior races."

> I think we now have sufficient population in our country for us to shut the door and to breed up a pure, unadulterated American citizenship . . . Who is an American? Is he an immigrant from Italy? Is he an immigrant from Germany? I would like for the Members of the Senate to read that book just recently published by Madison Grant, *The Passing of the Great Race*. Thank God we have in America perhaps the largest percentage of any country in the world of the pure, unadulterated Anglo-Saxon stock. . . . [15]

A comparison of the average number of immigrants arriving during the first two decades of the twentieth century and the 1924 quotas clearly illustrates the intent and the consequences of immigration restriction (Table 2-4).

The American Catholic community did not remain silent during the debate over immigration restriction. During WWI a group of prominent

Table 2-4. Average Number of Immigrants per Year: 1900–1919 vs. 1924 Quotas

	Avg. Per Year 1900–1919	1924 Quota
Total	727,488	164,667
Europe	627,899	142,483
Northern European Countries		
Ireland	39,718	28,567
Germany	25,147	51,227
Norway	13,101	6,453
Sweden	17,869	9,561
Sub-total	95,835	95,808
Southern - Eastern European Countries		
Hungary	62,446	473
Poland	n.a.	5,982
Russia	130,414	2,248
Italy	158,019	3,845
Greece	17,176	100
Sub-total	368,055	12,648

Catholic leaders met at Catholic University in Washington, D.C., in 1917, and formed the National Catholic War Council to support American troops fighting in Europe. After the war the council was renamed the National Catholic Welfare Conference (NCWC), involved "in federal, state, and local levels in Catholic activities concerning legislation, education, publicity, and social action."[16] In 1966 the NCWC was reorganized as the National Conference of Catholic Bishops (NCCB). Father James Burke, a Paulist priest, served as the first Director of the NCWC and, in 1919, established a Social Action Department to "Americanize" Catholic immigrants, mirroring the Pennsylvania Model of assimilation. NCWC, in 1924, sent a letter to Congress protesting the proposed immigrant restriction legislation:

> We respectfully protest . . . such a policy [quotas] is distinctly un-American: it is a departure from the enduring tradition of our country . . . She is strong enough to assimilate, in the future as in the past, the foreigners who will come to us a normally restricted immigration.[17]

The NCWC did not oppose all restrictions but vehemently opposed restriction based on country of origin.

With the passage of the immigration restriction in 1924, the Century of Immigration came to a close and the legislation represented an end to the Pennsylvania Model. For the next four decades, quotas by country of origin would be the deciding factor determining who could come to the U.S. with the proper "papers," who would be documented. After 1924, given the draconian quotas, both overall and by country, immigration declined dramatically (Figure 2-4). In the decades that followed, the Great Depression and World War II also contributed to the decline of immigration. Few people came to America; not until the 1960s did immigration resume on a large scale.

The quota system basically remained in effect until the Immigration and Nationality Act of 1965. If people in Italy or Hungary or Poland wanted to come to the United States, to reunite with family or for economic opportunity and they could not obtain one of precious few immigration visas, they could not come. Their only other choice—find a way to reach America, without documentation; to live in the promised land as an "undocumented" person.

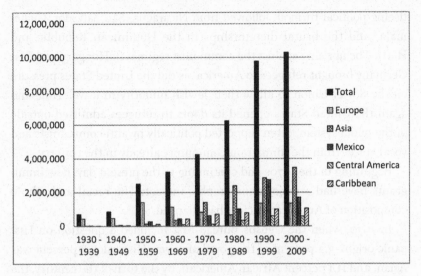

FIGURE 2-4. Persons Obtaining Legal Residence by Decade 1900–2009. (Source: U.S. Department of Homeland Security, *Yearbook of Immigration Statistics*, 2012. Census data reflects the changing demographic composition of the country.)

Immigration Reform: Unintended Consequences

In 1965 Congress made major changes to the country's immigration laws. Quotas were not abandoned but were changed to areas of the world rather than individual countries. Family reunification became an important criterion for obtaining a visa, as did preferences for highly skilled occupations and immigrants with college or advanced degrees. "Unskilled" workers in occupations with labor shortages could also be given preference; the latter reflected an ongoing need for agricultural workers to do the back-breaking labor in the fields and orchards and other dirty and dangerous jobs.[18]

What Congress did not anticipate was the dramatic shift in immigration patterns; a new wave of immigrants followed, not from Europe as many supporters of reform anticipated, but people from Asia, Mexico, Central America, and the Caribbean. America's post-WWI foreign policy and the Cold War led to numerous changes in immigration law. After America's wars in Asia, the Korean War, and the Vietnam War, Koreans, Vietnamese, and Cambodians who supported the United States were allowed to enter. The Cuban Communist revolution forced many to flee the island and find refuge in America. A similar wave of immigrants, fleeing political turmoil, followed from Nicaragua, San Salvador, Guate-mala, and the brutal dictatorships in the Dominican Republic and Hatti. The uprising against the communist regimes in Hungary and East Germany brought refugees to America, as did the United States pressure on the Soviet Union to allow their Jewish minority to leave. Time and again the United States opened its doors to refugees admitted outside of the quota system, often supported politically by anti-communists and vocal voices from the immigrant community already in the country.

Beginning in the 1970s and continuing to the present day, new immigrants have had a major demographic impact: The racial and ethnic composition of American society has changed.

In 1970, when the Census Bureau first included a question on Hispanic origin, 3.2 percent of the population was Hispanic, .8 percent was Asian, and 11.1 percent African American. By the turn of the century, the Hispanic population had increased dramatically from 8.9 million to 35.3 million and comprised 12.5 percent of the total population (Figure 2-5). In the next ten years the Hispanic population continued to grow and reached 16.3 percent of the total population in 2010, the largest minority group in the country.

Many Hispanics are Roman Catholics, and their presence has had a major impact on the Catholic dioceses across the country, especially

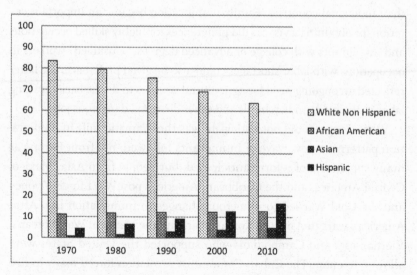

FIGURE 2-5. U.S. Population by Race and Hispanic Origin 1970–2010.

in the major cities and metropolitan regions where they live. A Pew Research Center study found that 68 percent of Hispanics identify themselves as Catholics.[19] Many prefer to practice in "ethnic congregations" that have Hispanic clergymen and Spanish-language services, and where a majority of congregants are Hispanic. In many inner-city neighborhoods Hispanic congregations have reinvigorated moribund Catholic parishes, originally constructed to serve European Catholic immigrants a century or more ago. Catholic grammar schools have reopened and high schools remain open as parents have elected to send their children to parochial schools, requiring daunting financial sacrifices for many. At Jesuit universities, the numbers of Hispanic students have increased significantly and often comprise the largest minority group on campus. Following the pattern of immigration from Europe in the nineteenth century, the United States today is home to many generations from Latin America.

Undocumented Immigrants

Post-WWII America sustained an unprecedented economic boom for thirty years, creating what the economist John Kenneth Galbraith described as the first society of mass affluence in history.[20] In the 1950s American businesses produced more than half of all manufactured products in the world, and millions of families achieved middle-class status, including legions of second- and third-generation Irish, German, Hungarian, and Italian Catholics. Galbraith's "Affluent Society" sustained full employment which led to labor shortages, especially in agriculture and low-wage service occupations.

During WWII Mexico and the United States negotiated a "temporary" contract labor program to allow Mexican workers to enter to provide agricultural workers and railroad laborers. The *Bracero* program allowed for 125,000 migrant laborers to be employed in the United States. The program officially ended in 1945, but under intense pressure from U.S. growers the program was extended, time and again, until 1963. An estimated 4.5 million Mexican *Braceros* labored as temporary workers, and despite often abysmal work conditions, many obtained a green card to legally remain in the United States. Given the extreme poverty in Mexico, other *Braceros* decided to stay as undocumented workers even in the face of the constant fear of deportation.

When the program ended in 1963, the Mexican migrant population in the country was established and the lure of a better life in the United States led to large scale border crossings, without documentation, as millions fled Mexico. Tens of thousands of migrants followed from other countries in Central America and South America, many without proper documentation, creating a moral and political crisis that persists to the present day. Other undocumented migrants arrived, not just from the Americas but from around the world. People entered as visitors and simply stayed joining relatives already here or moving to already immigrant communities across the country, repeating a pattern of "chain migration" that has characterized the entire history of immigration.

However, as the numbers of undocumented continued to increase, pressure mounted on Congress and the states along the border with Mexico to do something. Those opposed to immigration demanded that the government step up efforts to apprehend and deport anyone without proper documentation. The National Catholic Welfare Conference and later the National Conference of Catholic Bishops joined other religious and political leaders who presented a religious and moral argument for creating a program to allow the undocumented, under specific conditions, a path to legal status and citizenship.

From the 1980s on, Congress struggled to pass legislation to deal with the undocumented crisis (see Table 2-5).[21] As political power shifted between the Republican and Democratic parties, the emphasis swung back and forth between policing the borders and more aggressive deportation to immigration reform with a path to citizenship. No consensus emerged. In recent years political positions have hardened; immigration as an issue has joined the bitter "culture wars" that characterize our current political climate. Echoes of the Know Nothing Party, the Immigration Restriction League, and the eugenicists are heard today; the diversity of the new America is viewed as a threat. Despite how hard the immigrants work and the obstacles they overcome, just as the Irish, German, Scandinavian, and Italian immigrants did in the nineteenth century, they are viewed with suspicion. When first elected in 2008, President Obama listed immigration reform as one of his major objectives. Seven years later no comprehensive reform had been implemented; the one major piece of legislation, the DREAM Act of 2010, passed the House but failed in the Senate.

Table 2-5. Immigration Legislation: 1986–2010

Year	Act	Provisions	Category
1986	The Immigration Reform and Control Act (IRCA)	Employer sanctions program—penalties for hiring unauthorized worker.	Restriction
		Legalization—3 million undocumented—entered country prior to January 1, 1982.	Path to legal status
1990	The Immigration Act	Increased number of immigration visas annually from 290,000 to 675,000.	Pennsylvania Model
1996	The Illegal Immigration Reform and Immigrant Responsibility Act (IIRAIRA)	3–10 year ban on return to U.S. for undocumented deported.	Restriction
		Apply for asylum status within 1 year of arrival.	Restriction
		Local police deputized to act as immigration officials.	Restriction
2000	The Legal Immigration Family Equity Act (LIFE)	Expanded process for family reunification—immediate relatives of U.S. citizen—permanent residency.	Reform
		V-visa to reunite spouses & children of green card holder in U.S.	Reform
2010	The Development, Relief, and Education for Alien Minors, or DREAM Act* * not passed in Senate	Pathway to citizenship for undocumented brought to U.S. before 16 years of age, in U.S. for 5 years, complete high school, pass background checks.	Path to citizenship

Source: Center for American Progress.—"5 Major Immigration Laws that the House Passed in an Election Year"; www.americanprogress.org.

The DREAM Act provides a path to citizenship for a very specific sub-group of the undocumented: children brought to the United States before they were sixteen years of age, many when they were small children or infants. Often they do not learn of their status until they are in high school and some not until their senior year when they begin to fill out college applications that require a social security number or foreign student visa. Without proper documentation they are not eligible for any federal financial aid, as their parents cannot complete the required Free Application for Federal Student Aid (FAFSA) application. In many states they also cannot apply for state financial aid or qualify for in-state tuition. A significant majority of the undocumented students at Jesuit universities are "DREAMers," students who would qualify for the path to citizenship, if the DREAM Act of 2010 had become federal law.

The Undocumented at Jesuit Universities—The DREAMers

On Jesuit campuses the undocumented immigrants follow in the footsteps of generations of immigrants and their children from Ireland, Germany, Italy, and other European countries. These new immigrants believe that a Jesuit education is the key to achieving their American dream and the dreams of their parents. These students overcome enormous obstacles— educational, financial, and emotional—to complete their degrees even in the face of the fact that when they graduate they still will be without legal status.

Providing educational opportunity to all, including the undocumented, remains at the core of the Jesuit mission. A commitment to serving the undocumented reflects the principles articulated in Jesuit universities' Mission and Identity statements:

Fairfield University

. . . primary objectives are to develop the creative intellectual potential of its students and to foster in them ethical and religious values and a sense of social responsibility. Jesuit Education, which began in 1547, is committed today to the service of faith, of which the promotion of justice is an absolute requirement . . . . it welcomes those of all beliefs and traditions who share its concerns for scholarship, justice, truth and freedom, and it values the diversity which their membership brings to the university community.

Fordham University

. . . we believe that students have to be invited to wrestle with the great ethical issues of their time. We want them to be bothered by the real-ization that they don't know everything and bothered by injustice.

Gonzaga University

The Gonzaga experience fosters a mature commitment to dignity of the human person, social justice, diversity, intercultural competence, global engagement, solidarity with the poor and vulnerable, and care for the planet . . . . The common good and a just society cannot be attained without working to positively impact the state of the poor, the vulner-able, and those marginalized by society at large.

Providing opportunity for the undocumented comes with many chal-lenges, especially providing the financial aid that these students need to be able to attend college. Their immigrant parents often work in low-paying occupations, and finding the money to pay for a private education at a Jesuit university is daunting. Without a significant amount of finan-cial aid from each university's own resources, in the absence of federal and state aid, these students could not afford to attend a Jesuit university.

One example: at Fairfield University, as part of the commitment to op-portunity, the university established a community scholarship program which awards merit-based scholarships to the top graduating seniors at the public and parochial high schools in the City of Bridgeport, Connecticut. Bridgeport is one of the poorest cities in the United States. Among these outstanding students are those who are undocumented.

Supporting undocumented students is a challenge at Jesuit universities just as serving European immigrants was in the nineteenth century. Today administration, staff, and faculty clearly understand and are committed to the mission of providing opportunity for the undocumented (see Chap-ter 5). The undocumented students at Jesuit universities are a recent chapter in the history of Jesuit higher education in America. From the founding of Georgetown in 1789 to Fairfield University in 1942, the mission of these universities has been to provide an opportunity for all grounded in a moral and religious commitment to justice.

Notes

1. Oscar Handlin, *The Uprooted: The Epic Story of the Great Migrations That Made the American People* (Cambridge, Mass.: Harvard University Press, 1951; 2d enl. ed. 1973).

2. Passenger Act of 1819.

3. Susan Martin, *A Nation of Immigrants* (New York: Cambridge University Press, 2011).

4. See Taylor Anbinder, *The Five Points* (New York: Free Press, 2001).

5. http://www.bc.edu/offices/pubaf/about/history.html.

6. Emphasis added. http://www.fordham.edu/info/25693/our_story.

7. See Kerby Miller, *Out of Ireland: The Story of Irish Emigration to America* (New York: Elliot & Clark, 1994).

8. John Higham, *Strangers in the Land: Patterns of Nativism 1860–1825* (New York: Atheneum, 1963.

9. Howard Mumford Jones, *The Age of Energy: Varieties of American Experience, 1865–1915* (New York: Viking Press, 1971).

10. United States Department of Homeland Security, Office of Immigration Statistics, *Yearbook of Immigration Statistics: 2012*, Table 2.

11. Irving Howe, *World of Our Fathers: The Journey of the East European Jews to America and the Life They Found and Made* (New York: Harcourt Brace, 1976).

12. Jacob Riis, *How the Other Half Lives: Studies among the Tenements of New York* (Kessinger Publishing, 2004).

13. James Hennesey, *American Catholics: A History of the Roman Catholic Community in the United States* (Oxford University Press, 1981), 173, 187.

14. Madison Grant, *The Passing of the Great Race* (New York: Scribner's, 1921).

15. Ellison DuRant Smith, April 9, 1924, *Congressional Record*, 68th Congress, 1st Session (Washington, D.C.: Government Printing Office, 1924), vol. 65, 5961–5962.

16. *American Catholic History Classroom*, American Catholic History Research Center and University Archives, http://cuomeka.wrlc.org/exhibits/show/immigration/background/immigration-intro, accessed 5/8/2015.

17. Letter from Bruce Mohler, Director NCWC—Social Action Committee, to House Committee on Immigration and Naturalization, January 7, 1924, Catholic University Archives.

18. See Martin, *Nation of Immigrants*, 183; and Martin, "'A Nation of Immigrants': 1965–1994" for a comprehensive overview of post-WWII changes and modifications to immigrant law.

19. Pew Research Center, "Changing Faiths: Latinos and the Transformation of American Religion," April 2007.

20. John Kenneth Galbraith, *The Affluent Society* (New York: Houghton Mifflin, 1958).

21. See Martin, *Nation of Immigrants*, Chap. 10, 11, 12, and 13 for a detailed overview of political and legislative efforts to change immigration policies and law.

Table Sources

Table 2-1: Frederick Knapp, Immigration and the Commissioners of Emigration (New York: The Nation Press, 1820).

Table 2-2: U.S. Department of Homeland Security, Yearbook of Immigration Statistics, 2012.

Table 2-3: U.S. Department of Homeland Security, Yearbook of Immigration Statistics, 2012.

Table 2-4: U.S. Department of Homeland Security, Yearbook of Immigration Statistics, 2012.

3 Becoming Allies in Eradicating Long-Standing Legal Barriers

ANA NOBLEZA SISCAR AND SAHNG-AH YOO

Immigration policy in the United States related to undocumented students has been a front-burner political issue for at least four decades now. However, changes to permanent policies have been slow and, as a result, the laws and public policies surrounding these issues do not reflect current statistics and needs. Oftentimes unwitting children accompany moving families. Many of them end up becoming undocumented and growing up in the United States indistinguishable from their U.S. citizen peers culturally, geographically, and linguistically. Outdated laws and divided politics prevent such students from gaining legal status in the United States, and thus, displace them in their "own" country. Translated to a sense of displacement on campus, colleges often misunderstand the difficulties these students face and the support they need. With proper information and support, universities could be instrumental in paving a just and compassionate path to undocumented students' access and success in higher education and to a formal recognition of their "American identity" with citizenship status under the law. While the permanent fix relies on the passage of a comprehensive immigration reform by Congress at the federal level, universities have the opportunity to assume the role of an ally of undocumented students inside and outside the confines of their campus life.

This chapter aims to provide a streamlined account of the laws and policies most relevant to undocumented students in higher education. We begin by first contextualizing the legal discussion on educational institutions within a social justice framework, before describing the legal landscape of the education of undocumented students from K–16 (Kindergarten through College). In this section, we explore two specific legal policies that have greatly affected how undocumented students experience higher education: the 1996 Omnibus Immigration Laws and the Deferred Action for Childhood Arrivals (DACA). We then look forward and explore future trends of the legal landscape. Next we propose that universities have a role to play in paving a just and compassionate path to undocumented students' access and success in higher education, with or without comprehensive immigration reform. Finally, we conclude by posing a challenge to universities—how do your (in)actions on this issue define the ideals of a democratic society and an educational institution committed to social justice?

Social Justice, Democracy, and Higher Education

The definition of social justice has morphed to encompass not merely the distribution between socioeconomic divisions, but rather the recognition of the identities and societal worth of culturally defined groups.[1] The contemporary struggle for the recognition of social groups' identities and differences can find its resting place in our education system. For some, schools should remain uninvolved in political matters, neutral to biases, and limited to just teaching the facts of history. Cochran-Smith (2009) argues that "neutrality is impossible,"[2] especially within a democratic society that depends on civic deliberation and respect for differences. We have seen schools and colleges play important roles for social progress in the past, like the Little Rock Nine initiative in 1954. The Little Rock School Board was one of the first school boards to uphold the *Brown v. Board of Education* (1954) ruling and provide the first steps toward racial desegregation in our schools.[3] Little Rock Central High played a crucial role in the civil rights movement and will always be remembered for its initiative for social justice and heavy influence on its community.[4] In the same vein, colleges play a role in educating the community toward recognizing the identities and societal worth of undocumented students as uniquely defined groups who live among us, in giving undocumented students equal opportunities to participate in education, and in ushering their full inclusion in society. Universities' actions on these roles promote the ideals of life, liberty, and pursuit of happiness prescribed by our immigrant forefathers in the U.S. Declaration of Independence and the Constitution.

Higher Education Policies and Immigration Law

Education plays an important part in the United States' legacy of meritocracy. It is the most direct means of social mobility and fulfilling the ideals of life, liberty, and pursuit of happiness inscribed in the Constitution. With the changing globalizing economic landscape, higher education, in particular, has become more and more valuable with the skills it teaches and its correlation with income. Studies show that the difference in work-life earnings between workers with a high school diploma and those with a college degree is one million dollars.[5] With the increased stake in education in mind, this section presents a streamlined explanation of the United States' current laws on education as they relate to undocumented students, beginning with a brief overview of K–12 education before discussing the promising yet complicated nature of the Deferred Action for Childhood Arrivals (DACA) program within the college context.

K to 12 Education

The early '80s was a watershed in the education of undocumented students. The Supreme Court handed down the landmark case of *Plyler v. Doe* (1982),[6] which guaranteed a free public K–12 education to undocumented children on the basis of the Equal Protection Clause of the Fourteenth Amendment. This case affirmed the illegality of the efforts by various school districts across the country to bar undocumented children from attending K–12 public schools. According to Justice Brennan, the denial of education to some isolated group of children poses an affront to one of the goals of the Equal Protection Clause: the abolition of governmental barriers presenting unreasonable obstacles to advancement on the basis of individual merit.[7] He reminded us of the ruling in *Brown v. Board of Education* (1954)[8] when the Supreme Court said, "In these days, it is doubtful that any child may reasonably be expected to succeed in life if he is denied the opportunity of an education. Educating children, regardless of their immigration status, is essential for forming individuals who can function in society and contribute to the development of the United States."[9]

However, while the rationale of these pronouncements equally holds true for college education, the guarantee of *Plyler* stops at 12th grade and thus leaves a serious gap in its underlying principle of removing unreasonable obstacles to advancement on the basis of individual merit. The end of 12th grade separates the path of undocumented and documented students, activates the "illegality" of undocumented students, and magnifies the role of law in their lives.[10] As college tuition rises, they struggle trying to overcome legal barriers, including the increased documentation requirement in college and scholarship application processes, as well as prohibition from engaging in work supported by the federal or state governments (e.g., work-study grant).

College

Graduates across the United States continue to face legal barriers to access and success in college. Barriers include legal efforts to prohibit admission to colleges and universities, restrict access to financial and institutional aid, and prohibit professional practice licensing post-graduation. In the ensuing paragraphs, we describe two major legal developments that have shaped paths and roadblocks to higher education for undocumented students across the United States, and their actual and potential impact: the 1996 Omnibus Immigration Laws and the Deferred Action for Childhood Arrivals

THE 1996 OMNIBUS IMMIGRATION LAWS

In 1994, California passed Proposition 187 or the so-called Save Our State initiative that sought, among other actions, to prohibit undocumented students from accessing public education at any grade level, and prevent them from being admitted to postsecondary educational institutions by requiring these institutions to verify the immigration status of all enrolling students every semester. Although it was a state-specific measure, it spurred copycat legislations in many states. These were eventually ruled unconstitutional on the basis that they infringed on the federal government's exclusive jurisdiction over matters relating to immigration. However, it presaged the passage of two omnibus laws that pervasively regulate noncitizens' eligibility for state and federal benefits,[11] the 1996 Illegal Immigration Reform and Immigrant Responsibility Act (IIRIRA) and Personal Responsibility and Work Opportunity Reconciliation Act (PRWORA), which are still the current laws of the land. These laws sparked debates on the legality of admitting undocumented students to postsecondary institutions and their access to state financial aid and in-state tuition. The following discussion clarifies what these laws do and do not limit.

Effect on admissions. Neither IIRIRA nor PRWORA limit attendance to postsecondary institutions (private and public). U.S. Department of Homeland Security (DHS) clarified that admission into a public postsecondary educational institution is not one of the benefits regulated by IIRIRA and is not a public benefit under PRWORA.[12] It added that "the individual states must decide for themselves whether or not to admit illegal aliens into their public postsecondary institutions" as a matter of public policy or through legislation in accordance with federal immigration status standards.[13] At the time of this writing, only three states have laws or policies that restrict undocumented students' access to public postsecondary institutions—South Carolina, Alabama, and Georgia.

Effect on federal financial aid, state financial aid, institutional aid, and in-state tuition. Unlike admissions, financial aid is limited by IIRIRA[14] and PRWORA (PRWORA, § 401 [c] [1] [A], PRWORA; 411 [c] [1] [A]).[15] On the federal level, the laws foreclosed undocumented students' access to federal financial aid (PRWORA, § 401),[16] e.g., Pell Grants, Federal Supplemental Educational Opportunity Grants (FSEOG), Teacher Education Assistance for College and Higher Education (TEACH) Grants, and so on.

At the state level, the Omnibus laws mandate that state financial aid and in-state tuition are under state jurisdiction and legislative discretion.[17] Twenty states authorize the eligibility of undocumented students to in-state tuition rate through legislation, a resolution from the Board of Regents or Board of Governors for Higher Education, or a directive from the State Attorney General. These states are California, Colorado, Connecticut, Florida, Hawaii, Illinois, Kansas, Maryland, Michigan, Minnesota, Nebraska, New Jersey, New Mexico, New York, Oklahoma, Oregon, Rhode Island, Texas, Utah, and Washington. In addition, Virginia's Attorney General has allowed DACA grantees to access in-state tuition. In contrast, there are states, i.e., Georgia, Arizona, and Indiana, with laws that explicitly prohibit allowing undocumented immigrants to pay in-state tuition. According to Gonzales (2009), proponents of in-state tuition for undocumented students argued that policy allowing them to pay in-state tuition fee "has not precipitated a large influx of undocumented students, displaced native-born students, or been a financial drain on the educational system. In fact, these measures tend to increase school revenues by bringing in tuition from students who otherwise would not be in college" (as cited in Pérez, 2012).[18] In addition, five states—California, Minnesota, New Mexico, Texas, and Washington—give undocumented students access to state financial aid, and two states—California and Illinois—enacted laws that award them private scholarships administered by the state.

There are also reports of confusion between state financial aid and institutional aid. Institutional aid is financial aid set aside by colleges and universities from anticipated tuition revenue for use by needy students. In other words, it is set aside from students' own tuition dollars and, thus, clearly different from the taxpayer-funded state financial aid and not under state jurisdiction. Due to misunderstandings, there are universities that needlessly prevent undocumented students from accessing this type of institutional aid.

The patchwork of different and confusing state laws and policies results in uneven access to higher education for undocumented students across the United States. Even with the benefit of in-state tuition, institutional aid and/or state financial aid, inability to legally work denies them the means to fully support the cost of their education, especially considering their ineligibility for federal financial aid and that they most likely come from low-income families. This problem is partially, temporarily, and fragilely addressed for students who are eligible and have qualified as the result of DACA.

DEFERRED ACTION FOR CHILDHOOD ARRIVALS (DACA)

The DACA directive (U.S. Department of Homeland Security, 2012) offers a solution to the issue of legal employment as it enables a grantee to obtain work authorization, albeit temporary and limited. DACA is an act of prosecutorial discretion to defer removal of an individual.[19] Described as a "smart enforcement policy," DACA as envisioned prioritizes removal of criminal immigrants over law-abiding, young, productive immigrants, helping to unclog deportation courts.

A DACA grant also enables a grantee to obtain a social security number, driver's license if allowed by the state, and Advance Parole. Advance Parole is a permit to travel outside the United States for educational purposes, such as semester study abroad programs or academic research; employment purposes, such as overseas assignments, interviews, conferences, training, or meetings with clients; or humanitarian purposes, such as travel to obtain medical treatment, attend funeral services for a family member, or visit an ailing relative.[20] Moreover, once a DACA grantee reenters the United States on Advance Parole, the grantee will be considered "paroled" into the United States, which if coupled with an approved immediate relative petition on her or his behalf, makes her or him eligible to adjust status as a permanent resident of the United States with a path to citizenship. This holds true notwithstanding the "illegal entry" or the initial entry of the grantee into the United States without inspection. This transformative legal effect on status from undocumented to a legal permanent resident is rooted in Section 245 (a) of the Immigration and Nationality Act, which governs the discretionary adjustment of status for persons paroled into the United States and the guarantee given in the precedential case of *Matter of Arrabally and Yerrabelly* (2012).[21] This case guarantees that leaving the United States on Advance Parole was not really a "departure" that will trigger the unlawful presence bar, which prevents adjustment to permanent residency status unless resolved by a complicated waiver process. Unlawful presence bars prevent a person who has maintained unlawful presence in the United States for one year or more from coming back for ten years following departure from the United States, and a person who has unlawful presence for more than six months but less than one year from coming back for three years.[22]

Thus, DACA allows grantees to bypass many obstacles that had prevented them from being incorporated into society in a humane and productive way. In addition, a recent study shows that "DACA beneficiaries have experienced a pronounced increase in economic opportunities, and that these benefits appear to be the strongest for those attending four-year colleges and those with college degrees" (Gonzales and Bautista-Chavez, 2014, p.4).[23] According to a study published by the American Immigration Council (2014) at the one-year mark of DACA, approximately 60 percent of DACA recipients surveyed had obtained a new job, 49 percent had opened their first bank account, and 57 percent had obtained a driver's license since receiving DACA status.

However, only a subset of undocumented students is eligible for DACA. There are limitations based on age (under the age of 31 as of June 15, 2012), years of residency (have continuously resided in the United States since June 15, 2007, up to present time), presence in the United States (were physically present in the United States since June 15, 2012 and at the time of filing the DACA application; were in the United States before 16th birthday), educational attainment or service in the Coast Guard or Armed Forces of the United States, and commission of crime including three or more misdemeanors. The Obama administration attempted to remove some of these restrictions.

Constitutionality of DACA. On November 20, 2014, President Obama announced a new round of executive actions, which included an expanded DACA program that eliminated the age cap and reduced the required years of residency to be counted from 2010 instead of 2007. This means that students or graduates older than 30 years who were ineligible under the 2012 DACA could enjoy deferred action and other appurtenances of DACA status if they met other criteria. However, the day before the scheduled rollout of the expanded DACA program on February 18, 2015, a federal judge in Texas in the case of *United States* v. *Texas* (2015) temporarily blocked its implementation to deliberate not the legality of the program, but a technical rule concerning whether the administration followed the requirement for promulgating a rule change. This is not, however, the first attempt to challenge the DACA Program.

In *Crane v. Napolitano* (2012), several Immigration and Customs (ICE) Officers and Agents filed a case against Janet Napolitano, then Secretary of Homeland Security, after she rolled out the first DACA program in 2012.[24] They claimed that the program: violates the federal statutes requiring them to initiate removal proceedings when they encounter illegal immigrants who are not "clearly and beyond a doubt entitled to be admitted," and that any "prosecutorial discretion" can only be exercised after removal proceedings have been initiated;[25] and transgresses our constitutional separation of powers and the constitutional obligation of the executive to take care that the laws are faithfully executed.[26]

Whether granting deferred action to undocumented students is within the constitutional power of the president continues to hound the DACA program. Both DACA defenders and opposition cite the "Take Care Clause" or the "Faithful Execution Clause" of the Constitution.[27] This clause imposes a duty on the president to take due care while executing the laws, even if he disagrees with the purpose of the law.

Defenders of the constitutionality of DACA often base their interpretation of the "Take Care Clause" allowing the Executive Branch due discretion on its enforcement policies on the pronouncement made by Justice Kennedy in the pre-DACA case of *Arizona v. United States* (2012).[28] Justice Kennedy described the broad discretion exercised by the Executive Branch and immigration officials in deciding whether it makes sense to pursue removal at all. He even elaborated that discretion embraces immediate human concerns, which include whether the alien has children born in the United States, long ties to the community, a record of distinguished military service, or other equities. He further emphasized the implications of the president's discretionary decisions on United States' international relations. He explained:

> Returning an alien to his own country may be deemed inappropriate even where he has committed a removable offense or fails to meet the criteria for admission. The foreign state may be mired in civil war, complicit in political persecution, or enduring conditions that create a real risk that the alien or his family will be harmed upon return. The dynamic nature of relations with other countries requires the Executive Branch to ensure that enforcement policies are consistent with this Nation's foreign policy with respect to these and other realities.[29]

Perhaps, a clearer way of understanding the president's discretionary use of deferred action is by juxtaposing the DACA-type discretion with classic prosecutorial discretions in the criminal justice and administrative law fields. The Attorney General and United States Attorneys retain broad discretion to enforce the nation's criminal and administrative laws. They have this latitude as president's delegates to help discharge his or her constitutional responsibility to "take Care that the Laws be faithfully executed." In *Heckler v Chaney* (1985), the Court recognized that "an agency's refusal to institute proceedings shares to some extent the characteristics of the decision of a prosecutor in the Executive branch not to indict—a decision which has long been regarded as the special province of the Executive branch, inasmuch as it is the Executive who is charged by the Constitution to 'take Care that the Laws be faithfully executed.'"[30] It ruled:

[T]he agency must assess whether a violation has occurred, but whether agency resources are best spent on this violation or another, whether the agency is likely to succeed if it acts, whether the particular enforcement action requested best fits the agency's overall policies, and, indeed, whether the agency has enough resources to undertake the action at all. An agency generally cannot act against each technical violation of the statute it is charged with enforcing. The agency is far better equipped than the courts to deal with the many variables involved in the proper ordering of its priorities (pp. 831–832).[31]

On the other hand, groups opposing DACA view the "Take Care Clause" as "a requirement that the President ensures that 'the laws are executed, and that he or his agents do so with care.'"[32] While opponents concede that the Executive Branch retains broad discretion in allocating resources to achieve its priorities, allocation decisions cannot ignore congressional policies.[33] In *Crane v. Napolitano* (2012), the judge found that the federal statutes provide clearly defined standards for when immigration officers are required to initiate removal proceedings against undocumented individuals; accordingly, judicial review of the policy of the DHS is available to ensure that it complies with the laws.[34] Unfortunately, while the judge found that these substantive legal issues presented are "fit for judicial review" pursuant to the Declaratory Judgment Act, the federal appeals court dismissed the case for plaintiffs' lack of legal standing to sue over President Obama's 2012 DACA program, reasoning that the evidence that the agents or the state would be harmed was too speculative. This decision did remove a hurdle in the implementation of the 2012 DACA program, but it missed the opportunity to directly deliberate the substantive legality of the program, the omission of which presages more attacks against it in the future.

As of September 2016, a recent case on the constitutionality of DACA is the *United States v. Texas*, which reached the Supreme Court in January 2016. Despite a lack of constitutional legal action raised in the lower courts, the Supreme Court directed the parties to brief and argue whether President Obama's executive action violates the Take Care Clause of the Constitution. This presented an opportunity for a comprehensive decision on the constitutionality of DACA. However, the seat in the Supreme Court vacated by the death of Justice Antonin Scalia and

kept unfilled by Congress resulted in a 4-4 deadlock among the justices
that left this important discussion on hold.

Limitations of DACA. The incessant attacks on DACA probably contribute
to insecure feelings about the program. Since DHS started receiving DACA
applications on August 15, 2012, 669,019 initial applications were granted.[35]
Nevertheless, only roughly half of the DACA-eligible population filed their
applications, which raises the question: Why is the other half not filing?[36]
In addition, history and the fact that less than 9 percent of eligible Chinese signed up for DACA (Batalova, 2013) raise the possibility of lingering
distrust of the U.S. government. U.S. immigration law history is marred
with exclusion of specific nationalities.[37] The prohibition of Chinese laborers' immigration under the Chinese Exclusion Act (1882) is but one
example.[38] Others attribute the cause to cultural inhibitions. According
to Betty Hung, "In the Chinese community . . . there is such a community
culture of silence about this."[39]

Other possible reasons include the cost-prohibitive filing fee of $465,
inability to present documents such as those proving their continuous
presence in the country, lack of awareness about the program in the rural
areas and/or to populations of certain countries, fear of deportation for
themselves should their application get denied, fear of deportation for their
families because a DACA grant does not extend to their families,[40] and
uncertainty since a DACA grant "confers no substantive right, immigration status, or pathway to citizenship."[41] In other words, a DACA grant and
its appurtenant effects can be taken back anytime because they are not
rights that vest. United States Citizenship Immigration Services (USCIS)
confirmed in a DACA FAQ updated on October 23, 2014, that "DACA is
an exercise of prosecutorial discretion and deferred action may be termi-
nated at anytime, with or without a Notice of Intent to Terminate, at DHS's
discretion."[42]

Another serious limitation of DACA is that it does not remove the restriction from getting licensed to practice a profession imposed by
PRWORA (§ 401 [c] [1] [A]) to undocumented graduates.[43] Hence, DACA
grantees still face legal impediments in working as lawyers, doctors,
nurses, teachers, social workers, accountants, air pilots, electricians, and
other licensed professionals. Relevant to aspiring law practitioners, the
Supreme Court of California in the case of *In re Sergio C. Garcia on*

Admission (2014) concluded that a recently enacted state law removes any potential statutory obstacle posed by PRWORA to a successful undocumented bar examinee's admission to the practice of law in California.[44] However, it did not resolve the legality of working as a sole practitioner or independent contractor for lawyers who are undocumented, nor does it cover other professions and other states. Following California's example, Florida passed a law that allows unauthorized immigrants to be admitted to practice law. However, aside from the condition that the applicant has fulfilled all requirements for admission to practice law in this state, it imposes additional conditions such as the applicant: was brought into the United States as a minor; has been present in the United States for more than ten years; has received documented employment authorization from USCIS; has been issued a social security number; and if a male, has registered with the Selective Service System if required to do so.[45] While both California and Florida enacted statutes to override the prohibition in PRWORA to engage in the legal profession, a New York Appellate Court exercised the discretion authorized in PRWORA as a coequal branch of government in ruling that undocumented immigrants who have been granted a DACA relief may be admitted to the practice of law provided they otherwise, each individually, meet the standards for admission by which all candidates for admission to the practice of law are judged.[46] The court reasoned that undocumented immigration status, in and of itself, does not reflect adversely upon a person's general fitness to practice law, and the admission of the attorneys and counselors to the practice of law is the domain of the judicial branch. It reiterated the principle laid out in *Plyler* that condemnation on the head of an infant is illogical and unjust, and declared that it is unrealistic to expect that the applicant would leave the only country he has known since the age of five and return to a country with which he has little more than a connection by birth.

Unresolved Issues Perceived as Long-standing

Erecting barrier after barrier in the path of undocumented students and graduates to education, employment, practice of profession, and eventual citizenship is perceived as another facet of a long-standing opposition, often codified into law, toward the presence of "foreigners."[47] Over the course of history, the U.S. government has instituted various immigration policies that reflect a strong nativist influence. The Naturalization Act of 1790 limited naturalized citizenship to free white persons only.[48] Although the law was modified to include Africans almost a century later, it still excluded Asians and Latinos, who had to wait for the next century to qualify for naturalization.[49] In 1882, the federal government created its first explicit discriminatory law that prohibited entry of a specific ethnic working group on the premise that it endangered "the good order of certain localities."[50] The Chinese Exclusion Act targeted Chinese "skilled and unskilled laborers" from entering the country for ten years under penalty of imprisonment and deportation. The Act also affected Asians who had already settled in the United States; for example, any Chinese immigrant who left the United States had to obtain certifications for reentry, while being excluded from the path to citizenship, permanently alienating them from this country even as life-long residents.[51] When the ten-year period was over, nativist culture had not died down (and arguably, still lives on in the twenty-first century) and the Act was renewed in 1892. It was not until 1943 that the Act was reconsidered and repealed.[52] By then, the Immigration Act of 1924 sought to establish a distinct American identity by favoring native-born Americans over Jews, southern Europeans, and eastern Europeans in order to "maintain the racial preponderance of the basic strain on our people and thereby to stabilize the ethnic composition of the population."[53]

By the early 1960s, History.com reports that calls to reform U.S. immigration policy had mounted, thanks in no small part to the growing strength of the civil rights movement.[54] It explains that the growing public focus on equal treatment regardless of race or nationality led many to view the quota system of the Immigration Act of 1924 as regressive and discriminatory. Thus, in 1965, the new Immigration and Nationality Act (INA) abolished the national origins quota system and replaced it with a preference system that focused on reuniting immigrant families and attracting skilled labor to the United States. Thus according to the report, in the first five years after the bill's passage, immigration to the United States from Asian countries—especially those fleeing war-torn Vietnam and Cambodia—would more than quadruple. By the end of the twentieth century, the policies put into effect in 1965 had greatly changed the face of the American population.[55]

And while some treat undocumented immigration as an exclusively modern twenty-first-century problem, the United States has witnessed illegal entry throughout its history. Notably, in the 1980s, illegal immigration was a constant source of political debate as Canadian and Mexican immigrants entered the country by foot.[56] In response, the Immigration Reform and Control Act (IRCA) of 1986 legalized certain undocumented populations who entered the United States before January 1, 1982,[57] and had resided here continuously with penalty of a fine, payment of back taxes, and admission of guilt.[58] The law resulted in the grant of legal permanent resident status to 2.7 million undocumented immigrants, 48 percent of whom became naturalized U.S. citizens.[59] However, it left behind many undocumented immigrants who did not make the 1982 cutoff date, and many undocumented immigrants hesitated to come forward because of a fear of deportation. Over the years, undocumented immigrants increasingly took advantage of the 1986 IRCA.[60] Unfortunately, this coincided with the economic recession of the early 1990s, reviving nativist and xenophobic responses, which eventually led to state and federal laws encroaching on immigrants' rights to fair access to education, e.g., the IIRIRA, the PRWORA, and California's Proposition 187 discussed earlier in this chapter.

IIRIRA not only directly affected the students' access to education but it also increasingly criminalized immigration law which marginalized both the undocumented population and legal immigrants alike. For example, it expanded the definition of "aggravated felony" beyond the state laws' coverage to include crimes as minor as "shoplifting." Other laws such as the Antiterrorism and Effective Death Penalty Act of 1996 made the vague crime of "moral turpitude" a deportable offense. Thus, conviction of a crime considered as violating "moral turpitude" or "aggravated felony" for immigration purposes leaves one immediately deportable, without access to U.S. citizenship permanently, and crippled in terms of ability to legalize her or his immediate family's immigration status is concerned.

What we are seeing is a phenomenon called "crimmigration," where the area of criminal law has slowly become infused in the area of immigration law, which is typically an administrative law. This phenomenon has the consequence of unfairly creating "folk devils" out of immigrants or anyone perceived as immigrants. In fact, often, as in the case of the

Antiterrorism and Effective Death Penalty Act of 1996, preventing crimes and terrorism has been, "at least, on a discursive level of policy formation, the main driving force and justification" for these measures.[61] However, according to Stumpf, "[e]xcluding and alienating a population with strong ties to family, communities, and business interests in the United States fractures our society in ways that extend well beyond the immediate deportation or state-imposed criminal penalty."[62] Wittingly or unwittingly, they "fed a powerful vision of the immigrant as a scofflaw and a criminal that began to dominate the competing image of the benign, hardworking embodiment of the American dream."[63] The bidirectionality between criminalizing immigration law and racial prejudice impacts the undocumented population in more profound and nuanced ways. It amounts to an assault of the basic civil and human rights of immigrants.

While not the focus of this chapter, our history presents an important backdrop to the discussion and the dismantling of barriers that continue to hurt undocumented students and graduates. The issues faced by undocumented students today expose the ills of an outdated immigration system that carries the remnants of institutionalized discrimination against immigrants evident throughout our nation's history. Both Democrats and Republicans have taken aim at reforming the immigration policies in place, realizing that they have failed to keep up with the demands of globalized markets.

While recent developments involving DACA, state financial aid, and in-state tuition extend the impact of *Plyler* to undocumented college students and graduates a bit further, it is a limited success considering the number of immigrants who remain unqualified and the fact that half of the DACA-eligible population remains, out of fear, "unDACAmented." Whether the children who were raised in American schools on American food and in American homes decide to step out or stay in the shadows depends on how the United States begins to change its attitude toward its immigrants, in general. Absent a federal DREAM Act or a Comprehensive Immigration Reform that can pave a just and compassionate path to citizenship for the undocumented population, the unresolved issues surrounding their education, employment, practice of profession, family, and safety will persist and compound their struggle with their identities as adults. (See Table A-1 for the remaining key barriers that undocumented immigrants face.)

Trends in the Legal Landscape

While both the Republican and Democratic parties in Congress recognize immigration as an important and urgent matter, both politically and ethically, the United States government has failed to pass several of the bipartisan immigration reform bills that have come forward in the legislation. While human rights advocates may place the plight of immigrants as ethical arguments, Senate and House politicians have, in more recent years, launched a more "pragmatic" discussion surrounding immigration system reform in terms of benefits to the economy. In 2013, a group of four Republicans and Democrats presented a comprehensive immigration bill, S.744, that was a product of not only weeks of floor debate and committee rewrites but also months of private negotiations to produce legislation that would give the Senate a shot at passing immigration reform, something it was unable to do just six years ago. The bill would establish a 13-year pathway to citizenship for millions of undocumented immigrants, including several security benchmarks to obtain a green card.[64] In general, this bill saw a shift in the country's immigration policies away from a family-based system to one that focused more on work skills, requiring mandatory workplace verification system for employers but also including a new visa program for lesser-skilled workers.[65] While this passed in the Senate 68–32, it failed to pass in the House.

Given that the previously Democratic-led Senate had been more willing to pass these bills and the Republican-led House had not, it is reasonable for one to suspect that immigration reform is failing because of party disputes. The media has certainly painted a picture that corroborates, with headlines that read: "Republican leaders show little interest in returning to the issue after the Homeland Security fiasco."[66] On the other hand, there are others, like Fraga (2009),[67] who suggest that immigration policy-making is different from other issues because the ideas behind immigration reform can speak to different people in different ways, partially bypassing party lines. The question then becomes: Will this partisan-based voting persist into the future? Will the United States ever see true immigration reform?

This is a difficult question, in part because while congressional scholars have documented the rise in partisan polarization and its institutional implications,[68] there has been little attention to the substantive effects of polarization on specific policy domains, including immigration policy-making. Fennelly et al. (2013) conducted one of the few comprehensive analyses of the voting patterns on immigration policies for the past two decades.[69] They found that while votes on immigration policies cover many different topics, the most popular ones were on status ID, rights and benefits, and border security, with emphasis changing from year to year. In 1995–1996, for example, votes focused predominantly on restriction or expansion of rights and benefits, whereas in 2005–2012, votes focused on issues of border security. More significantly, the analysis points to President Obama's 2012 executive order as a main catalyst in pushing Congress to craft their own legislation or be left out of the immigration reform process again.

This suggests in the future, for any immigration reform bill to pass through both parts of Congress, a delicate balance of push and pull will be necessary on the part of the Executive Office, where the risk of swift executive action will push for legislative action but not alienate and foster aversive feelings in more restrictive, conservative Republicans. It also suggests that attempts at comprehensive policy changes may lead to an arduous and long road with little chance of success. Rather, tackling specific pieces of immigration reform one at a time may produce better results and foster enough bipartisan teamwork to eventually achieve a more understanding and humane approach to dealing with a significant, yet politically voiceless, community. With or without immigration reform, universities have the opportunity and capability to act.

Paving a Just and Compassionate Path

This section discusses why and how universities are instrumental in paving a just and compassionate path to undocumented students' access and success in higher education and to a formal recognition of their "American identity" with a citizenship status under the law. While the permanent fix relies on the passage of a comprehensive immigration reform by Congress, universities can assume the role of an ally of undocumented students inside and outside the confines of their campus life. An ally takes "personal responsibility for the changes we know are needed in our society" that are so often ignored or left to others to deal with.[70] As allies, universities can usher students and graduates out of a limbo that limits their academic potential, extracurricular engagements, and mobility in the social, economic, and political domains. In the process, universities can significantly shape the social justice ideals of our educational institutions and our democratic society.

Evidence points to a strong correlation between student success and the amount and quality of support a student receives in an educational institution.[71] The correlation is even higher for underserved populations like undocumented students. Since most undocumented students are first-generation college students, their parents can provide limited help to navigate the process of getting into and attending college.[72] Although families can provide critical emotional and verbal support to them,[73] adolescents and young adults, whether documented or undocumented, need experienced adults to guide them in navigating the college process. In the case of undocumented students, fear of deportation makes them wary of seeking support. They need trusted allies to navigate a path littered with barriers that are triggered by their lack of lawful immigration status. Better yet, they need allies who can help push for the eradication of these barriers.

The role of universities as allies of undocumented students starts from within. It begins with educating the university family—students, staff, faculty, leaders—with the legality of three fundamental aspects of university: education, privacy protection, and finance. First, it is legal to educate undocumented students from K through college. Second, staff does not have a legal obligation to report undocumented students to the government. This case should not be confused with the case of a person who came on an international student visa wherein a designated staff at university or college is required to report the termination of the student's academic status. Third, private scholarships are legal and a highly effective recruitment tool for attracting high-achieving undocumented students.[74]

Currently, most universities only have informal, ad hoc systems wherein a small number of university staff in admissions or financial aid offices deal with undocumented students in a "word of mouth network" or one that works "under the radar."[75]

Consequently, there is a lack of strong infrastructure and formal administrative support that could easily cause disruption, lack of information, and discontinuation of support to undocumented students should the staff resign, causing staff members to continue grappling with the legality of these three acts. Therefore, it is beneficial to have a formal system that handles undocumented students' college application and addresses their educational needs throughout their time in college. In addition, universities with law schools and who manage legal clinics can help students apply for DACA and determine if they have any paths to citizenship.

Aside from legal matters, undocumented students need crucial support in building a broader support network that gives them access to mentors or tutors; other allies, advocates, or sponsors; information on scholarships that do not require citizenship or residency; information on safe spaces where undocumented students could speak openly; and role models who could include a more senior undocumented student.[76] The student could be a DACA grantee who is now authorized to work or a former undocumented student who is now a U.S. citizen and a professional thanks to the path to citizenship provided by IRCA. Access to mental health professionals is also critical, considering that undocumented students have constantly faced insecurity, rejection, and other psychosocial issues in their lifetime. Jach and Storlie (2012) propose a collaborative social justice advocacy approach that enhances inter-professional collaboration among the student affairs practitioners and school counselors, the schools' connection with the families of undocumented students, and the community's understanding of the cultural framework from which these students and their families emerged.[77]

But the responsibilities of the university should not stop with implementing change within its premises on campus. The university holds a powerful voice in society that can help promote a just and compassionate path to undocumented students' access and success outside of those two or four years of higher education. Questions remain. What is our responsibility to undocumented students when they leave colleges and universities? Why do certain states have the prerogative to deny or limit undocumented students' access to public higher education institutions? The answers to these questions require a change in the laws, and the higher education community could be an influential change agent to push for the necessary reform. Universities are more than hubs of ideas. Institutions of higher education have become representatives of ideas—the questions raised, projects pursued, and policies changed are reflective of how society is now and could influence how society would progress in the future. Their credible stature in the community and on the issues makes them a potential linchpin in the broader immigration reform.

Reform should include a path to citizenship. Otherwise, it will result in a new underclass of noncitizens who are not free to vote and participate as full citizens. Reform should include a straightforward path without deceptively innocuous requirements of excessive fines and long waits. Reform should include a path to citizenship for the students' families, who are their most important source of emotional support. Reform should provide access to federal work-study and federal student loans. Reform should allow undocumented graduates to practice a profession. Reform would help businesses and the economy fill crucial needs. On the other hand, inaction will perpetuate the social injustice of preventing talented individuals from becoming fully integrated into the United States, the only place they have ever known as home. Universities have a historic opportunity to serve and live social justice and human rights.

Conclusion

Reform rests on the actions of those who change. The social injustice experienced by undocumented students in higher education is an issue that simply cannot remain unnoticed, forgotten, and ignored any longer. The question for universities is how will you confront the societal issue of our time that directly affects your students and your community? Neutrality is impossible.

Notes

1. N. Fraser, *Justice Interruptus: Critical Reflections on the "Postsocialist" Condition,* (New York: Routledge, 1997); C. E. North, "'Social Justice' in Education," 507–535.

2. Cochran-Smith, "Toward a Theory of Teacher Education for Social Justice," 445–467.

3. *Brown v. Board of Education* of Topeka, 347 U.S. 483 (Supreme Court of the United States May 17, 1954).

4. "Little Rock School Desegregation (1957)" (n.d.), http://mlk-kpp01 .stanford.edu/index.php/encyclopedia/encyclopedia/enc_little_rock_school _desegregation_1957/.

5. Julian, Work-Life Earnings by Field of Degree and Occupation for People with a Bachelor's Degree 2011, www.census.gov/prod/2012pubs/acsbr11-04.pdf.

6. *Plyler v. Doe*, 457 US 202 (Supreme Court of the United States June 15, 1982).

7. Ibid.

8. See note 3.

9. See note 6.

10. Pérez, *Americans by Heart*.

11. Aleinikoff, Martin, et al., *Immigration and Citizenship*.

12. Letter to Mr. Thomas J. Ziko, 2008: Sheriff (Ret.) Jim Pendergraph, July 24, 2008. Accessed October 20, 2013, from National Immigration Law Center: www.nilc.org/document.html?id=436.

13. Ibid.

14. Illegal Immigration Reform and Immigrant Responsibility Act of 1996 (1996). *8 U.S.C. § 1621*.

15. Personal Responsibility and Work Opportunity Reconciliation Act of 1996 (1996). Pub. L. No. 104-193, 110 Stat. 2105.

16. Ibid.

17. *Martinez et al. v. Regents of the University of California et al.*, S167791 (Supreme Court of California November 15, 2010).

18. Pérez, *Americans by Heart*.

19. U.S. Department of Homeland Security (2012). Exercising Prosecutorial Discretion with Respect to Individuals Who Came to the United States as Children. Washington D.C., United States.

20. USCIS (2013). "Consideration of Deferred Action for Childhood Arrivals Process," USCIS. Accessed October 23, 2013. http://www.uscis.gov/.

21. *Matter of Arrabally v. Yerrabally*, 25 I&N Dec. 771, BIA August 16, 2012.

22. Immigration and Nationality Act of 1952. (1952). Pub. L. No. 82-414, 66 Stat. 163.

23. Gonzales and Bautista-Chavez, *Two Years and Counting*, http://www.immigrationpolicy.org/sites/default/files/docs/two_years_and_counting_assessing_the_growing_power_of_daca_final.pdf.

24. *Crane v. Napolitano*, 920 F. Supp. 2d 724 (United States District Court Texas January 24, 2013).

25. Ibid.

26. U.S. Const. Art. II, § 3.

27. Ibid.

28. *Arizona v. United States*, 641 F. 3d 339 (Supreme Court of the United States June 25, 2012).

29. Ibid.

30. *Heckler v. Chaney*, 470 U.S. 821 (Supreme Court of the United States March 20, 1985).

31. Ibid.

32. Blackman, "Constitutionality of DAPA Part II," 201–269.

33. Ibid.

34. *Crane v. Napolitano*, 920 F. Supp. 2d 724 (United States District Court Texas January 24, 2013).

35. USCIS. (2015). USCIS Performance Data on DACA Applications. Accessed May 31, 2015, from http://www.uscis.gov/sites/default/files/USCIS /Resources/Reports%20and%20Studies/Immigration%20Forms%20Data /All%20Form%20Types/DACA/I821d_performancedata_fy2015_qtr1.pdf.

36. Taurel, "Why Are Some Still unDACAmented?" Retrieved from www .immigrationimpact.com

37. Batalova, Hooker, et al. (2013). "Deferred Action for Childhood Arrivals."

38. Yoo, "DACA: Where We Are and Where We Need to Be," 19–23.

39. Semple, "Advocates Struggle to Reach Immigrants."

40. Taurel, "Why Are Some Still unDACAmented?"

41. See note 19.

42. USCIS (2014). DACA Frequently Asked Questions. Accessed May 31, 2014, from http://www.uscis.gov/humanitarian/consideration-deferred-action -childhood-arrivals-process/frequently-asked-questions.

43. Personal Responsibility and Work Opportunity Reconciliation Act of 1996 (1996). Pub. L. No. 104-193, 110 Stat. 2105.

44. In re Sergio C. Garcia on Admission, S202512 (Supreme Court of California January 2, 2014).

45. Fla. Stat. § 454.021(3) (2014).

46. In the Matter of Application of Cesar Adrian Vargas for Admission to the Bar of the State of New York, 2015 NY Slip Op 04657 (Supreme Court of the State of New York Appellate Division, Second Judicial Department, June 3, 2015).

47. Rincón, *Undocumented Immigrants and Higher Education*.

48. Ibid.

49. LII (2015). Immigration Law: An Overview. Retrieved from Cornell University Law School: https://www.law.cornell.edu/wex/immigration.

50. National Archives and Records Administration (1989). Transcript of Chinese Exclusion Act (1882). Retrieved from http://www.ourdocuments.gov /doc.php?flash=true&doc=47&page=transcript.

51. Chinese Exclusion Act (May 6, 1882). Retrieved from Yale Law School Lillian Goldman Law Library: http://avalon.law.yale.edu/19th_century/chinese _exclusion_act.asp.

52. National Archives and Records Administration. (1989). Chinese Exclusion Act (1882). Retrieved from http://www.ourdocuments.gov/doc.php ?flash=true&doc=47.

53. Grant, *Conquest of a Continent*.

54. A&E Television Networks, LLC (2015). *U.S. Immigration Since 1965*. Retrieved from History: http://www.history.com/topics/us-immigration-since -1965.

55. Ibid.

56. Ibid.

57. Immigration Reform and Control Act of 1986 (1986). Pub. L. No. 99-603, 100 Stat. 3359.

58. Fennelly, Fraser, et al., "Preparing for Legalization."

59. Baker, Naturalization Rate among IRCA Immigrants. Retrieved from Department of Homeland Security: http://www.dhs.gov/xlibrary/assets /statistics/publications/irca-natz-fs-2009.pdf.

60. http://www.history.com/topics/us-immigration-since-1965.

61. Aas, "'Crimmigrant' Bodies," 331–346.

62. Stumpf, "The Crimmigration Crisis," 367–419.

63. Ibid.

64. Kim, "Immigration Reform Bill 2013: Senate Passes Legislation 68-32."

65. Ibid.

66. Everett and Kim, "Immigration Reform Looks Dead"; Meckler, "Bipartisan Senate Bills Would Increase Visas."

67. Fraga, "Building through Exclusion," 176–192.

68. Binder, *Stalemate*; Sinclair, *Unorthodox Lawmaking*.

69. Fennelly, Fraser, et al., "Preparing for Legalization."

70. Ayvazian, "Interrupting the Cycle of Oppression," 625–631.

71. Kuh, Kinzie, et al., *What Matters to Student Success: A Review of Literature*. Washington, D.C.: National Postsecondary Education Cooperative.

72. Pérez, *Americans by Heart*.

73. Ibid.

74. Fairfield University, Loyola University Chicago, and Santa Clara University Legal and Social Research Teams (2013). *Immigrant Student National Position Paper*.

75. Ibid.

76. Educators for Fair Consideration. (2012). Top Ten Ways to Support Undocumented Students. Accessed November 21, 2013, from www.e4fc.org /images/E4FC_EducatorTop10.pdf.

77. Jach and Storlie, "Social Justice Collaboration in Schools," 99–116.

References

A&E Television Networks, LLC. (2015). *U.S. Immigration Since 1965*. Retrieved from History: http://www.history.com/topics/us-immigration-since-1965.

Aas, K. F. "'Crimmigrant' Bodies and Bona Fide Travelers: Surveillance, Citizenship and Global Governance." *Theoretical Criminology* 15, no. 3 (2011).

Aleinikoff, T. A., D. A. Martin, H. Motomura, and M. Fullerton. *Immigration and Citizenship: Process and Policy* (7th ed.). St. Paul, Minn.: West Group, 2012.

American Immigration Council. *Two Years and Counting: Assessing the Growing Power of DACA*. Washington, D.C.: American Immigration Policy Center, 2014.

Arizona v. United States, 641 F. 3d 339. (Supreme Court of the United States June 25, 2012).

Ayvazian, A. "Interrupting the Cycle of Oppression: The Role of Allies as Agents of Change." In *Readings for Diversity and Social Justice*, 2e, ed. Maurianne Adams, Warren J. Blumenfeld, et al. New York: Routledge, 2010.

Baker, B. (December 20, 2013). Naturalization Rate among IRCA Immigrants: A 2009 Update. Retrieved from Department of Homeland Security: http://www.dhs.gov/xlibrary/assets/statistics/publications/irca-natz-fs -2009.pdf.

Batalova, J., S. Hooker, R. Capps, J. Bachmeier, and E. Cox. (2013). "Deferred Action for Childhood Arrivals at the One-Year Mark." Migration Policy Institute.

Binder, S. *Stalemate: Causes and Consequences of Legislative Gridlock*. Washington, D.C.: Brookings Institution Press, 2003.

Blackman, J. (2015). "The Constitutionality of DAPA Part II: Faithfully Executing the Law." *Texas Review of Law and Politics*, 20 (1).

Brown v. Board of Education of Topeka, 347 U.S. 483 (Supreme Court of the United States May 17, 1954).

Chinese Exclusion Act. (May 6, 1882). Retrieved from Yale Law School Lillian Goldman Law Library: http://avalon.law.yale.edu/19th_century/chinese _exclusion_act.asp.

Cochran-Smith, Marilyn. "Toward a Theory of Teacher Education for Social Justice." In *Second International Handbook of Educational Change*, 2009.

Crane v. Napolitano, 920 F. Supp. 2d 724. (United States District Court Texas January 24, 2013).

Dupuy, Alex, and Nancy Fraser. "Justice Interruptus: Critical Reflections on the "Postsocialist" Condition." *Contemporary Sociology* 26, no. 6 (1997).

Educators for Fair Consideration. (2012). Top Ten Ways to Support Undocumented Students. Accessed November 21, 2013, from www.e4fc.org/images/E4FC _EducatorTop10.pdf.

Everett, B., and S. M. Kim. (March 9, 2015). "Immigration Reform Looks Dead in This Congress." *Politico.*

Fairfield University, Loyola University Chicago, and Santa Clara University Legal and Social Research Teams. (2013). Immigrant Student National Position Paper.

Fennelly, K., Sara Fraser, S. Hang, M. Mahmood, and Y. Zhang. (2013). "Preparing for Legalization: Lessons from the Literature and In-Depth Interviews on Preparedness for Immigration Reform in New York State." New York: New York Immigration Coalition.

Fla. Stat. § 454.021(3) (2014).

Fraga, L. (2009). "Building through Exclusion: Anti-Immigrant Politics in the United States." In *Bringing Outsiders In: Transatlantic Perspectives on Immigrant Political Incorporation,* ed. J. Hochschild and J. Mollenkopf. Ithaca, N.Y.: Cornell University Press.

Gonzales, R. *Young Lives on Hold: The College Dreams of Undocumented Students.* New York: College Board Advocacy, 2009.

Gonzales, R., and A. Bautista-Chavez. *Two Years and Counting: Assessing the Growing Power of DACA.* American Immigration Council. Washington, D.C.: American Immigration Council. Retrieved June 24, 2014, from http://www .immigrationpolicy.org/sites/default/files/docs/two_years_and_counting _assessing_the_growing_power_of_daca_final.pdf.

Grant, M. *The Conquest of a Continent.* Abergele, UK: Wermod & Wermod Publishing Group, 1933.

Heckler v. Chaney, 470 U.S. 821. (U.S. Supreme Court March 20, 1985).

Hinojosa-Ojeda, R. *The Costs and Benefits of Immigration Enforcement.* Houston: Rice University's Baker Institute, 2013.

Illegal Immigration Reform and Immigrant Responsibility Act of 1996. (1996). 8 U.S.C. § 1621.

Immigration and Nationality Act of 1952. (1952). Pub. L. No. 82-414, 66 Stat. 163.

Immigration Reform and Control Act of 1986. (1986). Pub. L. No. 99-603, 100 Stat. 3359.

In re Sergio C. Garcia on Admission, S202512 (Supreme Court of California January 2, 2014).

In the Matter of Application of Cesar Adrian Vargas for Admission to the Bar of the State of New York, 2015 NY Slip Op 04657 (Supreme Court of the State of New York Appellate Division, Second Judicial Department, June 3, 2015).

Jach, E., and C. Storlie. "Social Justice Collaboration in Schools: A Model for Working with Undocumented Latino Students." *Journal for Social Action in Counseling and Psychology* 4, no. 2 (2012).

Julian, Tiffany. Work-Life Earnings by Field of Degree and Occupation for People with a Bachelor's Degree: 2011. Washington, D.C.: U.S. Dept. of Commerce, Economic and Statistics Administration, U.S. Census Bureau, 2012. www.census.gov/prod/2012pubs/acsbr11-04.pdf.

Kim, S. M. (June 27, 2013). "Immigration Reform Bill 2013: Senate Passes Legislation 68-32." *Politico*.

Kuh, G., J. Kinzie, J. Buckley, B. Bridges, and J. Hayek. *What Matters to Student Success: A Review of Literature*. Washington, D.C.: National Postsecondary Education Cooperative, 2006.

LII. (2015). Immigration Law: An Overview. Retrieved from Cornell University Law School: https://www.law.cornell.edu/wex/immigration.

"Little Rock School Desegregation (1957)." (n.d.). In Martin Luther King, Jr. and the Global Freedom Struggle Encyclopedia. Stanford, CA. Accessed December 30, 2013, from The Martin Luther King, Jr. Research and Education Initiative: http://mlk-kpp01.stanford.edu/index.php/encyclopedia /encyclopedia/enc_little_rock_school_desegregation_1957/.

Martinez, et al., v. Regents of the University of California, et al., S167791 (Supreme Court of California November 15, 2010).

Matter of Arrabally v. Yerrabally, 25 I&N Dec. 771. (BIA August 16, 2012).

Meckler, L. "Bipartisan Senate Bills Would Increase Visas and Green Cards for High-Tech Workers." *Wall Street Journal*. 13 January 2015.

National Archives and Records Administration. (May 6, 1882). Transcript of Chinese Exclusion Act (1882). Retrieved from http://www.ourdocuments .gov/doc.php?flash=true&doc=47&page=transcript.

National Archives and Records Administration. (1989). Chinese Exclusion Act (1882). Retrieved from http://www.ourdocuments.gov/doc.php?flash =true&doc=47.

North, C. E. "More than Words? Delving into the Substantive Meaning(s) of 'Social Justice' in Education." *Review of Educational Research* 76, no. 4 (2006).

Office of State and Legal Coordination/DHS. (July 24, 2008). Letter to Mr. Thomas J. Ziko, 2008: Sheriff (Ret.) Jim Pendergraph. Accessed October 20, 2013, from National Immigration Law Center: www.nilc.org/ document.html?id=436.

Pérez, William. *Americans by Heart: Undocumented Latino Students and the Promise of Higher Education*. New York: Teachers College Press, 2012.

Personal Responsibility and Work Opportunity Reconciliation Act of 1996. (1996). Pub. L. No. 104–193, 110 Stat. 2105.

Plyler v. Doe, 457 US 202 (Supreme Court of the United States June 15, 1982).

Rincón, A. *Undocumented Immigrants and Higher Education.* El Paso, Tex.: LFB Scholarly Publishing LLC, 2010.

Semple, K. "Advocates Struggle to Reach Immigrants Eligible for Deferred Action." *New York Times.* 9 December 2013.

Sinclair, B. *Unorthodox Lawmaking: New Legislative Processes in the U.S. Congress.* Washington, D.C.: CQ Press, 2011.

Stumpf, J. "The Crimmigration Crisis: Immigrants, Crime, and Sovereign Power." *American University Law Review* 56, no. 2 (2006).

Taurel, P. (October 23, 2013). "Why Are Some Still unDACAmented?" Retrieved from Immigration Impact: www.immigrationimpact.com.

U.S. Const. Art. II, § 3.

U.S. Department of Homeland Security. (2012). Exercising Prosecutorial Discretion with Respect to Individuals Who Came to the United States as Children. Washington D.C., United States.

USCIS. (2013). "Consideration of Deferred Action for Childhood Arrivals Process." USCIS. Accessed October 23, 2013. http://www.uscis.gov/.

USCIS. (2014). DACA Frequently Asked Questions. Retrieved May 31, 2014, from U.S. Citizenship and Immigration Services: http://www.uscis.gov /humanitarian/consideration-deferred-action-childhood-arrivals-process /frequently-asked-questions.

USCIS. (2015). USCIS Performance Data on DACA Applications. Retrieved May 31, 2015, from U.S. Citizenship and Immigration Services: http://www .uscis.gov/sites/default/files/USCIS/Resources/Reports%20and%20Studies /Immigration%20Forms%20Data/All%20Form%20Types/DACA/I821d _performancedata_fy2015_qtr1.pdf.

Yoo, S. A. (2015). "DACA: Where We Are and Where We Need to Be." *Roosevelt Review.*

Appendix

Table A-1. Remaining Key Barriers That Undocumented Students Face

DACA Grantee	Non-DACA Grantee/ Eligible	States Allowing for Certain Exemptions
Threat of deportation for family	Threat of deportation for self and family	
	Lack of employment authorization	

Table A-1. (*continued*)

DACA Grantee	Non-DACA Grantee/ Eligible	States Allowing for Certain Exemptions
	Lack of social security number	
Inability to practice a profession		California in the case of lawyers (whether non-employment permit holders can practice law as sole practitioners remains unresolved).
Lack of access to federal financial aid		
Lack of access to state financial aid		California, Minnesota, New Mexico Texas, and Washington (if requirements are met).
Lack of access to in-state tuition		California, Colorado, Connecticut, Florida, Hawaii, Illinois, Kansas, Maryland, Michigan, Minnesota, Nebraska, New Jersey, New Mexico, New York, Oklahoma, Oregon, Rhode Island, Texas, Utah, and Washington (if requirements are met). In Virginia, the Attorney General makes in-state tuition available to DACA grantees.
Uneven access to driver's license because access is determined state by state.		All states except Arizona and Nebraska allow DACA grantees to acquire a license (if requirements are met).
		A growing number of states (including California, Connecticut, Illinois, New Mexico, Utah, and Washington) have a procedure in place for the issuance of driver's license to undocumented population regardless of DACA status.
Risks associated with leaving the country even if advance parole can be obtained	Risks associated with leaving the country and advance parole cannot even be obtained	
Revocability of DACA Grant		
Absence of path to citizenship and lawful immigration status		

4   *Alma Mater, Mater Exulum.* Jesuit Education and Immigration in America

A Moral Framework Rooted in History and Mission

MICHAEL M. CANARIS

Here at our sea-washed, sunset gates shall stand
A mighty woman with a torch, whose flame
Is the imprisoned lightning, and her name
Mother of Exiles. From her beacon-hand
Glows world-wide welcome . . .

—Emma Lazarus, "The New Colossus"

An Opening Word

This chapter explores both the history and commitment surrounding 225 years of Jesuit higher education in the United States to provide what we have called the moral framework of this study, and examines the connection between the institutions so many in the Association of Jesuit Colleges and Universities (AJCU) network call their "alma mater" and the "mother of exiles" (in Latin *mater exulum*) as described in Emma Lazarus's famous poem. Have the Jesuit colleges and universities in the United States of America actually been places which "glow with world-wide welcome?" What elements in our collective history and in the contemporary interpretation of themes related to the distinctive spirituality taught on our campuses can put the intentions of the founder of the Jesuits, St. Ignatius of Loyola, into practice—which by objective standards have changed not only education patterns, but the history of the world—in touch with Lazarus's own grand and sweeping vision? And why should such an intersection matter to us today?

To begin, it is important to note that, to varying degrees, virtually all of the twenty-eight schools in the United States which constitute the AJCU umbrella organization had as one emphasis in their earliest years the education of first- or second-generation immigrant populations in the U.S.[1] This fact then informed our research strategies and helped us orient the resultant findings presented here to highlight, rediscover, and apply anew a profound truth: that Jesuit higher education shares a mission and commitment across generations to provide access to education; and in the U.S. context, especially to help immigrant families have an opportunity to earn their share of the American dream. In this chapter I have two goals related to this truth: (1) exploring the history of the Society of Jesus in the United States in terms of its relationship to immigrant populations, and (2) discussing contemporary themes which make such a continued commitment to the often excluded and underappreciated population of migrant students viable and fruitful today. By doing so, I hope to articulate the unique contribution this research sought to make in terms of understanding the role of mission-driven educational institutions in societies today.

An Honest Historical Analysis

As part of our study, we worked with twenty-five Jesuit college presidents to craft a public statement which contained in its text the following claim:

> [W]e recognize that the history of Jesuit institutions of higher education in this country is inextricably linked to first- and second-generation immigrant populations. Our schools have in the past been unique places of opportunity for some of the most disenfranchised and marginalized members of American society.[2]

Many excellent books have been written on the history of individual institutions—from Fordham to Boston College, Gonzaga to Wheeling Jesuit, Georgetown to the various Loyolas, and so on. But no meta-narrative has been constructed, of which we are aware, that deals with the Jesuit collegiate network's relationship with immigrant populations in America, although some influential work has been done on related histories by Gerald McKevitt and Raymond Schroth.[3] Here I hope to provide as broad and variegated a picture of this topic as possible by garnering relevant examples from a variety of historical sources to argue that such a unique relationship as described by the presidents' statement does in fact exist, while minimizing the limitations of (a necessary) particularity in selecting relevant anecdotes and testimonials which support this idea. It is very clear, both from the direct interactions of our research team and from the data we have collected around the country, that this particular dimension of the mission of Jesuit education matters in a deep and personal way to many on our campuses. Although some would likely argue that such a focus is not (and should not be) the purview of Jesuit, Catholic colleges.

In order to face such critiques, let us first here offer what would seem to be some rather grave counter-examples to at least the spirit of the presidents' claim above. First, an unsettling account of institutional xenophobia from the annals of Gonzaga's history in the Pacific Northwest:

> [In 1887, a] few days after the beginning of the school year Father [Joseph] Joset appeared with two Indian boys. He informed Father President that he wanted to register them as resident students of the new college. The answer he received indicates that the policy of the new school had been greatly altered since it was first conceived. "No," Father [James] Rebmann said, "we do not receive Indian students. The school is exclusively for American boys." "Well, you call those Americans," Joset snorted. "What about these Indian boys? Surely they are Americans, they were born in the country and have a prior right before anyone else."[4]

At the time, Joset's arguments did not prevail, and the "non-Americans" were barred entrance.

There were cultural precedents for such attitudes, even within the Society of Jesus itself. Centuries earlier, even as revered a figure as Francis Xavier was not particularly open to equity of accessibility, at least in terms or ordination and its related educational and formative preparation, for as his letters make clear, he was hesitant to welcome indigenous peoples to the Society of Jesus because of his notions of European social superiority.[5] And as has often been noted, for a period, the Jesuits participated in and profited as a body from being one of the largest collective slaveholders in the United States.[6] John Carroll, the founder of the earliest Jesuit institution of higher learning in America, once detestably quipped, regarding potential converts among the men and women owned as property by the Jesuits, that "Diamonds are sometimes found in dunghills."[7]

As such cases make painfully obvious, the idealized visions of educational accessibility, due process, fairness, and equality have not been universally applied with objectivity throughout history, and that includes within the network here being discussed. Though these accounts don't deal with immigrants *per se*, they make clear the unevenness with which the most marginalized were offered access to education and opportunity in the past. While such issues are perhaps not, technically speaking, part of voluntary "migration" histories, the relationship of the Society of Jesus to these and other marginalized communities, one clearly pockmarked with missteps and lamentable practices, is undoubtedly germane to the discussion at hand. The problematic nature of these realities was particularly evident here in the New World, whose discovery had raised a whole slew of theological, practical, political, and other unforeseen difficulties for the European mindset in the Age of Exploration and the subsequent centuries. And as with virtually every institution that has survived here for more than a few decades, the relationship between the Society of Jesus and the society of immigrants which constitutes our national and continental tapestry is a complex one.

Without shying away from these deplorable realities, our argument here is that, in fact, a unique and positive contribution of Jesuit higher education toward migrant, first-, and second-generation American populations *does* exist, which can speak to the contemporary immigration debate raging in the academy, pews, halls of congress, and dinner tables of our country today. As we will come to see, much of this relationship is rooted in the historical founding of the AJCU schools in the nineteenth and twentieth centuries (of course also including John Carroll's flagship Georgetown, dating to slightly earlier in 1789).

In 1964, the Jesuit Educational Association conducted a national survey of knowledge and opinion regarding Jesuit higher education. One of the comments cited in their study claimed at that time that the national image of Jesuit education "includes the notion of discipline, difficulty, intellectualism, awareness of modern research and progress, and a tendency to do something about this in the practical world of today that will manifest the leadership ability of the student."[8] In 1986, the International Commission on the Apostolate of Jesuit Education published a document entitled *The Characteristics of Jesuit Education*, which included among its descriptions of Jesuit education terms such as "world-affirming," "curriculum centered on the person and personal relationships (*cura personalis*)," "faith that does justice," and exhibiting "particular concern for the poor."[9] Mirroring this is the AJCU's own mission and apostolate statement of 2010, which emphasized their goal to "prioritize the education of . . . often vulnerable and underserved students."[10]

From where did the commitment and characteristics laid out in these statements originate, and what, if anything, do they have to do with immigration? The Jesuits have long been recognized for their dutiful efforts at missionary work among uneducated and impoverished peoples and have often been characterized as especially concerned with those deemed outcasts. They earned this reputation for their efforts prior to the faulty, sanitized accounts of history, which tend to privilege white Anglo-Protestant founding fathers, especially in terms of religious history and mission. The fabricated and quite prevalent idea that Christianity arrived in the New England and Mid-Atlantic colonies first on Puritan ships, and moved southward and westward over the following decades or centuries is patently false. As John Leary, S.J., points out in the somewhat melodramatic language of 1950s biography: "Before anyone had ever dreamt of Jamestown or Plymouth Rock, these men in black soutanes had pushed their way into Georgia. They had settled on five different spots in Florida, had ventured into the Carolinas, and had reddened the soil of Virginia with their blood . . . . Actually the Jesuits were a foundation only fifteen years old [after being approved by Pope Paul III in 1540] when they sent their men to the New World. They have been in America ever since."[11]

But since Jesuit education is not originally or primarily an American enterprise, its roots concerning this commitment to the "underserved" (*not* "undeserved") extend even beyond this New World context. Consider the esteemed Spaniard Juan Alfonso de Polanco, Secretary to Ignatius and subsequent Generals of the Society of Jesus for almost thirty years, who in the late sixteenth century gave some of the following reasons for the establishment and proliferation of Jesuit schools in Europe: "poor boys, who could not possibly pay for teachers, much less for private tutors, will make progress in learning and that their parents will be able to satisfy their obligation to educate their children." Thus, those "who are now only students will grow to be pastors, civic officials, administrators of justice, and will fill other important posts to everybody's profit and advantage."[12] In the earliest days, the schools being founded by the Society, from Messina to Majorca to the Roman College, were at Ignatius's insistence, open to students of every social class without distinction because they were generously endowed and did not charge tuition. The movement toward wealthier student populations in the immediately subsequent years was, according to John O'Malley, "far, far from the original intention, never actualized in the degree usually attributed to it, and insofar as it occurred was the result not so much of deliberate choices as of the special nature of the humanistic curriculum [saturated with philosophy, Latin and Greek literary classics, and an appreciation of eloquence]."[13] Though the educational landscape shifted, the Jesuits never abandoned their commitment to the poor, the sojourner, or as so many were themselves, the exile.

As Jesuit education developed into and then in the wake of the Ratio Studiorum in 1599, it sought to transcend the provincialism of nationalist identity.[14] It was common practice that students from varied backgrounds, locations, and social classes studied together. In his text on their earliest educational endeavors, Michael Foss points out: "The Jesuits took great care that their schooling should reflect the internationalization of the Society . . . . At Jesuit schools, the students had the chance to observe that strange animal, the foreigner, and measure him against the official propaganda. And since nationalities were treated equally under the church, individuals, too were given an equal opportunity to prove worthy and respectful sons of the church."[15] (The chance for daughters to do the same was a later development.) To keep this accessibility and internationalization a priority, "the schools were to cost the Society nothing—except time and manpower—and the pupil nothing."[16] Their own constitutions included the stern commandment: "No obligations or conditions are to be admitted that would impair the integrity of our principle, which is—To give freely what we have received freely."[17] We know that such approaches to tuition changed over time in order to make the system sustainable, as it became more institutionalized around the world, and as the face of that "manpower" eventually shifted in more recent decades from scholastics and priests to an increased presence of lay collaborators and employees. But the underlying commitment to providing opportunity for the disenfranchised remains a central theme which links Jesuit education today with its earliest period.

From the nascent days of the U.S., the Society of Jesus played an integral role in its development on a wide variety of fronts. Jesuits who crossed seas or borders to come here, like Andrew White (England), Isaac Jogues (France), Eusebio Kino (Italy), Jacques Marquette (France), Pierre-Jean de Smet (Belgium), John Bapst (Switzerland), and Michael Nash (Ireland), all obviously immigrants, were pioneers and trailblazers who were moved in diverse ways and with radically different charisms and expertise to help lay the intellectual, spiritual, and in many cases sociopolitical and organizational foundation for what would become the United States as we know it today.

The fusion of Ignatian spirituality and renaissance humanism, along with the growing mission of international education which, while a bit sedentary for Ignatius's original vision of his company, had become so much a part of the Society in the intervening years, crossed the Atlantic along with the meager possessions of refugee, émigré, and/or missionary Jesuit priests and brothers in the seventeenth, eighteenth, and nineteenth centuries. While that earliest college on the banks of the Potomac housed both English- and American-born Jesuits, St. Louis University was run by Belgians; Alabama, Kentucky, and New York had schools launched by Frenchmen; Woodstock and the seminary in Maryland were run by Neapolitans; and Jesuit schools of the Mid- and Far West had German, Italian, and other immigrant populations in their classrooms and administration from the earliest days.[18] The founding community at Fordham University in the Bronx was made up of 19 Frenchmen, 11 Irishmen, 6 Canadians, 3 Germans, and 1 Englishman, Spaniard, Belgian, Haitian, and Czechoslovakian, with only 3 American-born Jesuits. In fact, the first rectors of all but two of the twenty-one current AJCU schools founded in the nineteenth century were immigrants.[19]

This multiculturalism provided the American Jesuit schools with a rich and contoured understanding of important themes like "universality," "home," and "mission" right from their earliest days. Many of their own had sought refuge in this land of the Mother of Exiles, especially in the wake of the Society's suppression and restoration in the 1700s. The uniquely traumatic ordeal the order had undergone at the hands of their influential and wealthy enemies, when those suspicious of the Society in Portugal, France, and Spain convinced Pope Clement XIV to suppress the Jesuits, helped them recognize the need to carry such an initiative forward both during and after their forced exile in so many cases. New geographical *and* pedagogical contexts provided ample means of reenvisioning their work after the Society's official restoration in 1814.[20]

Their own history and that of the relationship between Catholics and Protestants in our nation led to the schools being perceived by others—and sometimes even envisioning themselves—as standing apart "socially, organizationally, and ideologically from native academies."[21] Yet, they wanted to assimilate in some important ways, so as to make the colleges themselves culturally appealing and to reach the maximum number of people. McKevitt points out through his reading of Philip Gleason, "The resulting push and pull between their desire to retain a distinctive identity and their need to serve the society [lowercase "s"] for which they existed has been (and remains) an ongoing tension within Jesuit universities."[22]

McKevitt goes on to describe the period in which most of these institutions arose: "Students came from all economic classes. St. Xavier College, a New York commuter school, drew the sons of working-class families because its location in the center of Manhattan's developing mass transit system made it economically and geographically accessible. Founders intended Boston College to be a 'low tuition college for day scholars.' 'No student, however poor, is refused admission because he is unable to pay tuition' officials reported in 1899, 'and of the four hundred young men registered in the college, scarcely more than half do so.'"[23]

By the time the nineteenth century came to a close, sons of immigrant families were finding their way into Jesuit classrooms across the country, often alongside native North Americans from Alaska to the Mexican border, all aspiring to forge paths of upward mobility because of the opportunities a Jesuit education provided. As one Santa Clara alumnus put it, "Whether native or Eastern, Mexican or South American, English, French, or Italians, Catholic or Protestant, Jew or Gentile, they were Santa Clara boys."[24] As will be made clear in the following chapters of this volume, the same Santa Clara University continues to lead the nation in some of these efforts toward greater access for the most vulnerable and excluded today through a program called the Hurtado Scholars.

Thus, the historical origins of the Society of Jesus, the development of their apostolates into the most successful international educational network the world has ever seen, and the complex challenges faced by immigrants, asylum-seekers, refugees, and interconnected members of an increasingly shrinking and globalized world are inextricably interwoven. In the sixteenth century, St. Ignatius famously claimed the most effective way to catechize, transform, and set the world on fire was to "Go in through another's door, so as to lead them out through yours." Meeting people in need where they are has always been a primary focus of the Society of Jesus. For hundreds of years, the classrooms of Jesuit colleges and universities have been filled with immigrants, on both sides of the desk and chalkboard. Today is no exception. The Golden Door of opportunity to the American dream has been and is still being offered to countless immigrant, first-, and second-generation families through their efforts, though sometimes through channels that, while demonstrating authentic interpersonal care and commitment, are fragile, tenuous, and frankly in many cases uninformed about the nuances of many of the attendant issues involved with students who are new immigrants. It is an important, if underappreciated, cultural, spiritual, and historical heritage of the network of Jesuit schools which needs to be re-emphasized and discussed openly in these times of vitriolic debate on immigration and related issues. Our campuses, from administration to facilities, from faculty and staff to students and alumni, need to be given the opportunity to learn more about their own institutional past and the rich patrimony they inherit as members of our intentionally diverse communities, and to forge ahead with new strategies and techniques for ever-better serving one another, with an eye toward those who are navigating the always difficult waters of higher education with the added challenges associated with immigration.

A Contemporary Arena for Applying Jesuit Principles

To move this analysis from the historical context to a more contemporary exploration of the theme as to why immigration and Jesuit education are realities still intertwined and mutually informative to one another, and how best to envision these paths forward, we turn first to the current Pope Francis, formerly known as Jorge Bergoglio. When then-Provincial of the Jesuits in Argentina, the future pope made an important administrative decision at the Colegio del Salvador in Buenos Aires, an institution then composed of two parallel bodies: one where children of privilege paid for an education and another non-tuition-paying one for those who could not afford the fees, but sought to rely on the generosity of the Society to teach their children. Without informing either sets of parents he was doing so, Bergoglio merged the two bodies, so that all the students went to class together.[25] His commitment to the underprivileged continued with his time as Archbishop of Buenos Aires, where he was tireless in his support of migrant communities in the poorest areas of the country, known in dialect as *villas miserias* (literally "towns of misery"), and often spoke out against injustice and corruption which doomed local people to a life of intolerable suffering. Such concerns obviously did not end with his election as pontiff, but have perhaps even intensified with the global awareness that comes from leading the universal Catholic Church. His first papal visit outside of Rome was to Lampedusa, the island "borderland" of Europe, and he has time and again brought the issues of migration, human trafficking, and the "globalization of indifference" to the fore of his papal teaching.[26] He has said that the trials of migrants pain him as would a "thorn in [his] heart."[27] There are a number of thematic areas from which we can suppose the current Jesuit pope is drawing his inspiration on this front, and related insights into the American context in which Jesuit education can be seen as offering our academic progeny both nourishment (the literal meaning of *alma mater*) and refuge (*mater exulum*).

First and foremost, Jesuit spirituality agrees with wider Catholic social teaching in asserting that believers and the church as a whole should strive to work for the *common good. The Compendium of the Social Doctrine of the Church* defines this as "the sum total of social conditions which allow people, either as groups or as individuals, to reach their fulfillment more fully and more easily."[28] It argues that society must keep in mind the "good of all people and of the whole person" and that the "human person cannot find fulfillment in himself, that is, apart from the fact that he exists 'with' and 'for' others."[29] Such themes intersect almost verbatim with two hallmarks of Ignatian pedagogy: commitment to *cura personalis* and to an explicit hope to cultivate "men and women for others." All of these obviously are rooted in an even more fundamental reality, namely, that of the dignity of every human person regardless of race, creed, birthplace, residential status, or documentation. *Cura personalis*, and its dedication to formation of the person (here understood as a student) to flourish not just intellectually but holistically and its concomitant commitment to mold graduates who are civically and morally engaged with their surroundings, thirsting for justice and willing to critique situations of disempowerment or marginalization, can all be read as having direct correlates to the immigration issues this current volume explores.

As part of the events surrounding this research project, we partnered with the Ignatian Solidarity Network to put some of these principles into action, promoting a "faith that does justice." With their help (particularly through the tireless coordination of Christopher Kerr, the organization's executive director), we were able to arrange for sixty undergraduate students from around the Jesuit network throughout the United States to travel with us to Washington, D.C., both to participate in the presentation of our research findings and to meet personally with either their House and/or Senate representatives to advocate for immigrant rights in higher education. Some of these students were themselves undocumented, which exhibits incredible courage and conviction to speak out regarding a claim to their share of the American dream. However, many others were students born in the United States (some of quite privileged backgrounds) who cared about the struggles being faced by their friends, peers, and classmates, or who simply saw the issue as a moral and social one having an impact on their lives and their nation. This was quite inspiring to those of us involved in the project from different angles, be it researchers or participating staff, administrators, and organizers. Our sessions and exchanges—with university presidents and politicians or simply among small groups of students—where so many shared their stories and concerns, hopes, and fears, engaging one another in authentic encounters which expanded each others' intellectual, social, and spiritual horizons, were resonant of why Jesuit education remains a formative element in the self-identity and priority in the lives of so many alumni after their graduation.[30]

Much of the form and content of these authentic and direct encounters rooted in relationships center on solidarity, the Catholic intellectual virtue which espouses the interconnectivity and interdependence of all human beings. The Second Vatican Council made clear that "One is the community of all peoples, one their origin, for God made the whole human race to live over the face of the earth. One also is their final goal, God."[31] The pope has carried such a vision forward, not only in terms of our common home as in his encyclical *Laudato Si'*, but also specifically in terms of migrants, when it comes to fostering what he has called a "church without borders."[32]

Besides being a guiding principle for social living, solidarity with one another is also a primary moral virtue connected to the practice of justice. As St. Thomas Aquinas puts it, a moral virtue is a habit that comes from action and repetition, and in so doing, becomes somehow incarnated in the practitioner.[33] Solidarity as promotion of justice is a virtuous way of thinking and acting which propels one to cultivate a habit of working and caring for the common good of all humanity irrespective of their national origins or legal status. It promotes the union of all people, including but not limited to the poor and weakest, to enhance flourishing and public discourse. This has long been a driving principle behind the mission of Jesuit education and to the specific apostolates related to it.

Other related Jesuit themes that guided our moral and ethical framework for the project included St. Ignatius's call to seek and find God in all things, and the description of the Ignatian vocation as being "contemplatives in action." These interrelated concepts lead us to argue that our moral and political lives necessitate informed reflection and active engagement in our world. It is not and has never been the goal of Jesuit education to foster a flight into the sacristy when problems of injustice, hatred, or intolerance present themselves. Rather, students and graduates of these institutions are called to recognize the transcendent dimension in every element of life, and to work accordingly to serve the human family, to be "contemplatives in action" oriented toward and tireless in their efforts for a better present and future. In 1993 Jesuit Superior General Peter-Hans Kolvenbach, S.J., penned a letter regarding Ignatian pedagogy in which he described the goal of educators in the Jesuit network as producing students excelling in "competence, conscience, and compassionate commitment." This implies that in whatever field our graduates choose, they should be willing and able to coordinate their ambitions and successes with a greater, transcendent focus on the good, the beautiful, and the true both metaphysically speaking, and as concretely expressed in familial, professional, and social life. The success or failure of such a goal turns on the ability to cultivate in students an appreciation and development of their own cognitive and moral agency in ever-changing contexts and situations.

Pope John XXIII's encyclical *Pacem in Terris* makes clear the Catholic position on migration: "[E]very human being has the right to freedom of movement and of residence within the confines of his own State. When there are just reasons in favor of it, he must be permitted to emigrate to other countries and take up residence there. The fact that he is a citizen of a particular State does not deprive him of membership in the human family, nor of citizenship in that universal society, the common, world-wide fellowship of men."[34] Our project sought to take such a principle and articulate it in terms of our contemporary situation, an example of what Ignatian education has long called *eloquentia perfecta*. This phrase is intended to encourage students to wrestle with matters of morality, civic duty, and prudential judgment in areas both theological and humanistic, and to provide tools to articulate with "perfect eloquence" the results of this rigorous critical analysis for the benefit of the church, academy, and world. The Jesuits have long sought to cultivate the rhetorical skills to express with precision, persuasion, and grace one's most deeply held convictions. The current initiative explored in this volume has sought to provide for the world of higher education and the wider nation a cogent and ethical argument "to support our students—both documented citizens and not—as full members of our campus communities and of society at large, where their voices and personal narratives deserve to be acknowledged," as the shared presidential statement puts it.[35]

The last Ignatian theme to be discussed here can likely best be understood as a necessary element in all that has been traced in this chapter, and a unifying capstone to the entire project when understood though these lenses. St. Ignatius of Loyola's Spiritual Exercises have always been appreciated for endorsing the virtue of prayerful discernment when it comes to decision-making at all levels, both private and corporate. It has sometimes been described as having a focus on being *attentive, reflective,* and *charitable* ("caritative") in weighing potential paths forward on a given matter, but always experienced through a disciplined and rigorous sifting process to determine the proper course of prudential action and its relevant meaning for one's life and for the world at large. While it has vocational overtones in the Jesuit system, Roger Haight, S.J., has recently described the core components of this process as having potentially wider applicability, even among non-believers.[36] Pope Francis has affirmed the indispensability and centrality of discernment in the Jesuit way of thinking and living, and seems to support such a broad appreciation of its intrinsic value. He is then worth quoting at length:

Discernment takes time. For example, many think that changes and reforms can take place in a short time. I believe that we always need time to lay the foundations for real, effective change. And this is the time of discernment . . . . A Jesuit is a person who is not centered in himself. The Society itself also looks to a center outside itself; its center is Christ and his church. So if the Society centers itself in Christ and the church, it has two fundamental points of reference for its balance and for being able to live on the margins, on the frontier. If it looks too much in upon itself, it puts itself at the center as a very solid, very well 'armed' structure, but then it runs the risk of feeling safe and self-sufficient. The Society must always have before itself the *Deus semper maior*, the always-greater God, and the pursuit of the ever greater glory of God, the church as true bride of Christ our Lord, Christ the king who conquers us and to whom we offer our whole person and all our hard work, even if we are clay pots, inadequate. This tension takes us out of ourselves continuously. The tool that makes the Society of Jesus not centered in itself, really strong, is, then, the account of conscience, which is at the same time paternal and fraternal, because it helps the Society to fulfill its mission better . . . .

Only in narrative form do you discern, not in a philosophical or theological explanation, which allows you rather to discuss. The style of the Society is not shaped by discussion, but by discernment, which of course presupposes discussion as part of the process. The mystical dimension of discernment never defines its edges and does not complete the thought. The Jesuit must be a person whose thought is incomplete, in the sense of open-ended thinking.[37]

While recognizing that the value and *imago Dei* present in every human life, whether "native-born" or immigrant, is unequivocal and straightforward, we of course recognize that immigration reform and its relationship to higher education is a complex reality, with many attendant dimensions, causes, variables, and consequences. The Jesuit "way of proceeding" and contribution to the conversation about immigration unfolding in the public square, with its historical antecedents as outlined above, must be rooted in a realization that discernment is necessary in determining the best possible course of action in terms of the former, current, and future students whose lives we hope to touch and better, and on the wider society in which they live, move, and wield various types of influence.

Conclusion

Christians and Jews read in the Book of Leviticus the unambiguous demand levied upon believers: "When a stranger resides with you in your land, you shall do him no wrong. You shall treat the alien among you as if he were native-born, for you were aliens yourself in the land of Egypt; I am the Lord your God" (Lev 19:33–34). The member institutions of the AJCU have a specific mission and obligation to work for the promotion of justice, as informed by the biblical mandate put forth in such passages in the scriptures. From the time of Ignatius himself, Jesuits have seen in education a path "to help souls," as he put it succinctly. Our work in this project has examined the cultural, historical, and political context in which we find ourselves today in terms of mirroring this intention.

Applying such a goal to today's debates has led us to a number of conclusions. First, as the presidents' statement asserted: "We oppose public policies that separate human families living peaceably in our midst, especially those involving students and/or minors, and urge all citizens to recognize and support those inhabitants of our nation who seek to contribute more fully to civic life and the common good through education and personal development."[38] Justice, mercy, and charity—which are always interconnected virtues—demand care for those immigrant families who live, work, and raise their children among us, many of whom lack even the most basic legal protection or subsistence living standards, to say nothing about social mobility. Surrounded by young people and students, many of whom had ties to the Jesuit University of San Francisco, former Auxiliary Bishop of San Francisco Robert McElroy (since named Bishop of San Diego) articulated the moral demands laid upon believers in a public gathering at City Hall: "The religious communities stand with the undocumented on [their efforts at rights involving work and education] not merely out of solidarity, not merely out of love for them, not merely out of a sense that this is a terrible marginalization which occurs in our society, but because at the very core of religious belief is the understanding that all of us are the children of the one God who has made us one family, and that documented rights are a fundamental human right which we ignore and deny at our peril as a nation."[39] Though Jesuit colleges of course welcome students of all faiths and none, the institutions themselves are formed by and rooted in such ethical and religious worldviews, and as such, Bishop McElroy's perspective finds authentic patterns of resonance in the findings and moral framework of our study.

Second, the history of Jesuit higher education traced above makes clear that the twenty-eight Jesuit colleges in the U.S., to varying degrees, have always prioritized and continue to prioritize vulnerable and underserved students, including immigrants and children of immigrants. For four and a half centuries, the Jesuits have sought to live and minister at the interface between church and culture. For the purposes of this exploration, the focus has largely been on their efforts at doing so in the United States. The critique of unjust social structures and pathologies in the political system which routinely lead to xenophobia, nativism, or neo-Know-Nothingism represent crucial arenas where Jesuit education can continue to live at this cultural frontier and mold the future.

Finally, the hallmarks of Jesuit education include unwavering commitment to Catholic social teaching and the common good, *cura personalis*, solidarity and the promotion of moral virtue, seeking God in all things, and helping form "men and women with and for others" and "contemplatives in action." All of this involves a conscientious, active, and attentive dedication to discernment in both spiritual matters and the prudential applications of living them out in our individual lives and the public square. We argue that the immigration crisis in this country, understood of course not in terms of their arrival but rather our oftentimes failed responses as a church and nation to appreciate them as brothers and sisters and not statistics, proves one place, among many, where Jesuit education can serve as a vanguard in informing and helping to shape discourse by making a substantive contribution from a principled Catholic perspective. Our work, as a morally-committed endeavor, has sought to accomplish such a goal. We consistently and strenuously reaffirm our commitment to this process and to allowing ourselves to be inspired. Interestingly, roughly 10 percent of the members of Congress have undergraduate or advanced degrees from AJCU schools. Life in the public square should, and in many cases does, reflect the good being done by so many on our campuses to stand in solidarity with all students, immigrant and not.

When Emma Lazarus wrote "The New Colossus," about the new Statue of Liberty erected a few miles from where Fordham and St. Peter's Universities already existed, there was, as there is now, nativist and parochial criticism about its message. Lazarus had been deeply troubled by the ongoing persecution of eastern European and Russian Jews and by the Chinese Exclusion Act of 1882, a law severely restricting immigration to the United States.[40] Her sonnet ultimately linked the Statue forever in the American imagination with those "huddled masses" who arrive here from elsewhere generation after generation. I have here used her less familiar allusion to the "Mother of exiles" to ask if it can inform the approach we have taken to our research, mission, identity, and communities. The land that served as such a Mother to so many exiles associated with Jesuit education, members of that Society and in the intervening years of all societies, is today in yet another period of turmoil when it comes to recognizing the rights and dignity of those "yearning to breathe free." Without denying the multifaceted challenges associated with immigration policy and its related socioeconomic, security, and governance concerns, our research has been framed by a moral duty to see what so many call our *alma mater* anew through the lens of this *mater exulum*. Our research findings argue that if the whole Jesuit network of higher education in the United States were to become more fully engaged in the challenges and issues of undocumented students, an engagement rooted in the history and principles of Ignatius and his followers through the years, then other colleges and universities could be emboldened with their own unique senses of mission and identity to exercise new models of leadership in related areas. Through its research and broad support, this study has sought to explain the current situation and practices at Jesuit institutions surrounding some of the most vulnerable members of our society and to examine the concerns and perceptions of students, staff, faculty, and alumni on critical issues related to their development, well-being, flourishing, safety, and contribution to society. We have tried to present a deeper understanding of the complex lives of undocumented students with the hope that our research will generate more public compassion for them, a compassion that has its roots in who we collectively have been as a network, and who we are now called to be.

Notes

1. Wheeling Jesuit University is a notable exception. While it has a unique identity and mission focused to a large degree on native-born, first-generation college students in Appalachia, even that institution is not divorced from many

of the commitments to the marginalized and to social mobility, which will be discussed here.

2. AJCU presidents' statement—January 2013. Accessed July 11, 2015, www .fairfield.edu/immigrantstudent.

3. See for instance Gerald McKevitt, S.J., "Jesuit Schools in the USA, 1814–c.1970," in *The Cambridge Companion to the Jesuits*, ed. Thomas Worcester (Cambridge: Cambridge University Press, 2008) 278–297; and Raymond A. Schroth, S.J., *The American Jesuits: A History* (New York: New York University Press, 2007).

4. Wilfrid P. Schoenberg, S.J., *Gonzaga University, Seventy Five Years* (Spokane, Wash.: Gonzaga University, 1963).

5. See Thomas M. Cohen, "Racial and Ethnic Minorities in the Society of Jesus," in *The Cambridge Companion to the Jesuits*, ed. Thomas Worcester (Cambridge: Cambridge University Press, 2008), 199–214, at 206.

6. For more on this, see the Jesuit Plantation Project through Georgetown University.

7. Schroth, *American Jesuits*, 71.

8. *Findings and Implications of a National Survey of Knowledge and Opinion of Key Groups Regarding Jesuit Higher Education in the U.S., Volume III: Selected Verbatim Comments of Participants* (Greenwich, Conn.: Nowland and Company, March 1964).

9. *The Characteristics of Jesuit Education, 1986.* Produced by the General Curia of the Society of Jesus, Borgo Santo Spiritu, 5, 00193, Rome Italy, December, 1986.

10. 2010 AJCU Mission and Apostolate Statement.

11. John P. Leary, S.J., ed., *I Lift My Lamp: Jesuits in America* (Westminster, Md.: The Newman Press, 1955), ix.

12. John W. O'Malley, S.J., "How the First Jesuits Became Involved in Education" in *The Jesuit Ratio Studiorum: 400th Anniversary Perspectives*, ed. Vincent J. Duminuco, S.J. (New York: Fordham University Press, 2000), 66. See also O'Malley, *The First Jesuits* (Cambridge, Mass.: Harvard University Press, 1993), esp. 200–242.

13. O'Malley, "Became Involved in Education," 67.

14. For more on the Ratio Studiorum, the official pedagogical system at the heart of Jesuit education for centuries, see the full text itself, available online in English at www.bc.edu/sites/libraries/ratio/ratio1599.pdf, accessed July 11, 2015. Also helpful is Robert Schwickerath, S.J., *Jesuit Education: Its History and Principles Viewed in Light of Modern Educational Problems* (St. Louis, Mo.: Herder, 1903). Of course, "modern" here is a relative term when considering the Ratio Studiorum was already in use for three hundred years at the time of this work's publication. It still inspires programs on Jesuit campuses today,

notably the University of Scranton's Special Jesuit Liberal Arts (SJLA) honors cohort.

15. Michael Foss, *The Founding of the Jesuits* (London: Hamish Hamilton, 1969), 176.

16. Ibid., 164.

17. See Thomas Hughes, S.J., *Loyola and the Educational System of the Jesuits* (New York: Scribner's, 1901), 67.

18. McKevitt, "Jesuit Schools in the USA," 278.

19. For more on this, see Schroth, especially 58–76.

20. For more on this period, see Robert E. Scully, S.J., "The Suppression of the Society of Jesus: A Perfect Storm in the Age of 'Enlightenment,'" *Studies in the Spirituality of Jesuits* 45/2 (Summer 2013): 1–42.

21. McKevitt, "Jesuit Schools in the USA," 278.

22. Ibid., 279.

23. Ibid., 281.

24. Ibid., 282.

25. Paul Vallely, *Pope Francis: Untying the Knots* (London: Bloomsbury, 2013), 50.

26. See for instance Pope Francis, *Homily in the Salina Quarter of Lampedusa*, 8 July 2013. http://www.vatican.va/holy_father/francesco/homilies/2013 /documents/papa-francesco_20130708_omelia-lampedusa_en.html, accessed July 11, 2015, and his Message for the 2015 World Day of Migrants and Refugees, where he calls for a "church without borders [*fronteras*], mother to all." Of related note is his commitment to end the scourge of human trafficking, which involves forced migration. See the *Joint Declaration Against Modern Slavery*.

27. Pope Francis, *Homily in the Salina Quarter of Lampedusa*, 8 July 2013. Accessed July 11, 2015, http://www.vatican.va/holy_father/francesco/homilies /2013/documents/papa-francesco_20130708_omelia-lampedusa_en.html.

28. *Compendium of the Social Doctrine of the Catholic Church*, 164. The footnote to this definition alludes to related sources: Second Vatican Ecumenical Council, *Gaudium et Spes*, 26: *AAS* 58 (1966), 1046; cf. *Catechism of the Catholic Church*, 1905–1912; John XXIII, Encyclical Letter *Mater et Magistra*: *AAS* 53 (1961), 417–421; John XXIII, Encyclical Letter *Pacem in Terris*: *AAS* 55 (1963), 272–273; Paul VI, Apostolic Letter *Octogesima Adveniens*, 46: *AAS* 63 (1971), 433–435.

29. *Compendium*, 165. The gendered language is obviously cited directly from the text.

30. Interestingly, roughly 10 percent of the members of Congress are included in this group, having undergraduate or advanced degrees from AJCU schools.

31. *Nostra Aetate*, 1.

32. See his Message for the 101st World Day of Migrants and Refugees (3 September 2014).

33. Summa Theologica (I–II, q. 64).

34. *Pacem in Terris*, 25.

35. AJCU presidents' statement.

36. See Roger Haight, *Christian Spirituality for Seekers: Reflections on the Spiritual Exercises of Ignatius Loyola* (Maryknoll, N.Y.: Orbis, 2012). Other key resources in the tradition on discernment include Karl Rahner, "The Ignatian Logic of Existential Knowledge: Some Theological Problems in the Rules for Making an Election in St. Ignatius's Spiritual Exercises," abbreviated in English in *The Dynamic Element in the Church* (New York: Herder and Herder, 1954), and Jules J. Toner, *A Commentary on St. Ignatius's Rules for the Discernment of Spirits* (St. Louis, Mo.: Institute of Jesuit Sources, 1982).

37. Pope Francis, "A Big Heart Open to God," interview in *America* 209 (30 September 2013):14–38.

38. AJCU presidents' statement.

39. See USF's web page for their Office of Diversity Engagement and Community Outreach, https://www.usfca.edu/studentlife/undocumented, accessed July 11, 2015.

40. For more on the Chinese Exclusion Act, see John Soennichsen, *The Chinese Exclusion Act of 1882: Landmarks of the American Mosaic* (Santa Barbara, Calif.: Greenwood, 2011). On Lazarus's writing of the sonnet, see Alexandra Socarides, "The Poems (We Think) We Know: Emma Lazarus's 'The New Colossus,'" *Los Angeles Review of Books*, April 2, 2013, http://lareviewofbooks .org/essay/the-poems-we-think-we-know-emma-lazaruss-the-new-colossus, accessed July 11, 2015.

5 Getting, Staying, and Being in College

The Experiences of Students

LAURA NICHOLS AND MARIA GUZMÁN

This chapter presents the experiences of undergraduate students at Jesuit colleges and universities in the United States based on interviews with twenty-five enrolled students at six of the twenty-eight private, non-profit Jesuit colleges and universities in the U.S. who were undocumented at the time of the interview. The six schools include two in the western region of the U.S., two in the Midwest, and two in the East. Together, the six institutions represent the breadth and diversity of Jesuit institutions, from a research university with undergraduate and graduate programs, a law school, and a medical school, to an undergraduate focused college with a large number of commuter and part-time students.

Research on the transition to adulthood for this population of immigrants, often referred to as the 1.5 generation because they were brought to the U.S. as children, is limited. A key issue that has been identified for this group is the change in legal status that occurs when students go from being legally enrolled in high school (because of protections provided in *Plyler v. Doe*) with access to the same rights and privileges of other students at the school, to having no protections once they graduate and turn 18 and their legal status becomes their own issue.[1] As Rumbaut and Komaie state, "Immigration to the U.S. is quintessentially the province of the young. Six out of seven immigrants arrive in early adulthood or as children" (p. 62).[2] To further complicate the issue of legality, many of the students we interviewed lived in mixed-status families, having younger siblings who were born in the U.S. and are thus citizens. As a result, the fear of deportation of one or both parents, and themselves, loomed over them not only as a personal fear, but also about what would happen to their younger citizen siblings if any of them were deported.[3]

This was not an abstract fear. Our interviews took place during a time of intensified frequency of deportations by the Obama administration, increasingly restrictive laws in some states such as Arizona (a few students grew up in that state), and (another) failed DREAM Act in Congress. The interviews were conducted just before the passage of DACA, which allows current students who have been authorized with temporary work permits to be employed on campus, participate in internships, and work legally in the U.S., at least as long as the temporary order is in place.

In addition, students dealt with issues related to racism and their classmates' lack of knowledge about immigration laws and how citizenship was obtained. While these issues were persistent throughout their educational trajectories, they became more pronounced while in college and transitioning to adulthood.[4]

Thus students' experiences profiled here give us insight into the experiences of hard-working students pursuing uncertain futures and encountering career-limiting laws under the constant fear of deportation. We start with a discussion of students' experiences coming to the United States followed by a focus on college: getting in, challenges to staying in college, what it is like to be in college while undocumented, to thoughts about moving on after graduation. We end with suggestions for colleges from students themselves.

Coming to the U.S.

Most students came to the U.S. with at least one member of their families. The majority came when they were toddlers or young children, while two of the twenty-five came when they were teenagers. Some came on tourist visas and others came to the U.S. illegally. Said Sandra, a student whose family initially came over on a visa when she was nine years old, "And we stayed here, and I think we came here early August, and then they just enrolled us in school. I was very confused; I thought we were going to go back. And we haven't gone back ever since."

While students grew up as fully American, one student Mara, reflected, "Everybody that moves here [from Mexico], when you're from a small town and you want to go back, it's always like, 'it's going to be short term, it's going to be short term' but then your kids start to grow up and their life is here, and you have an okay life here, and you do want to see your family members, but your life is already kind of here. It's harder to make the move to go back."

Because many students arrived to the U.S. as young children, they often did not understand their legal status. And every student had a different experience of finding out they were not authorized to legally reside in the U.S.; some students "always knew" in theory, but it was not until they wanted to go on school trips, get a driver's license, or apply for college scholarships that it really sank in that their futures and options would be limited because of their status. In many ways our data mirror what Gonzales found with college-goers who were undocumented in the interviews he conducted from 2003–09.[5] Students usually found out or only truly understood their legal status while applying to college and/or for financial aid.

Patricia said, "It wasn't until junior year when my mom, I was trying to apply to FAFSA and all that and then I realized that this was going to be a really big obstacle. Not having a social security number. That's when I just started, for some reason I didn't get depressed; I just kind of realized that I had to just keep going. I'd done so much work. I wasn't just going to not go to college." Supportive teachers helped Patricia work through the obstacles to applying. She said that although this situation did not depress her, she saw friends "when they found out they were undocumented, they weren't driven, they actually got really depressed and they stopped going to school, and they stopped just caring about education."

Patricia had the unique situation of both of her parents being residents, a younger sister who was a citizen, and only herself and another sister were undocumented. Her mom had been going back and forth to see her parents in her home country and Patricia happened to be born abroad. "Because most of my family is documented, we never talked about the issues because they can travel, they can get a job . . . when we were growing up my mom would coach me and tell me to tell people that I was born in this hospital in this city." Patricia indicated that she thought on some level the story of being born in the U.S. at that particular hospital was reality and she believed it until her senior year in high school.

Two of the twenty-five students were completely unaware of their status until just before starting college. For Teresa, it was only after her parents had given her a tax identification number to put for her social security number on the federal financial aid form and she was notified that the number did not work, that her dad sat her down and explained her status. She explained,

So, I had to fill out the FAFSA and I was like late, and I'm like, how do you fill it out? I had already sent my information, and then I got an email sent back to me and they are like, oh, your Social Security number is not working, so I thought that was interesting, so I told my dad and he was like, oh, like print out that letter that they sent you, and he's like, oh, I'll talk to the lawyers and I was like, what? Why do you need to talk to them about it? And he just kind of just did his own thing and I didn't think anything of it, and like the following day he like sat me down and he was like, okay, well, this is the situation, like you don't have papers. And I was like, okay, like . . . It really did not hit me. And I was like okay. And he was like, so you can't apply to financial aid. So, I was like, okay. And he was like, well, he was like, don't worry, like we'll fix it, like you're fine, like he joked about it, he was like, you know the only thing you can do now is like wait until your sister turns twenty-one or go back or get married, in a very humorous way, so I was like, okay, well, I'm not going to get married or any of that, so I'll just wait, and so, and then my dad was like, you know, you are eighteen now so you are no longer considered under our care, so there is nothing we can do for you now that you are technically legally an adult. So, that was kind of how I found out. It was interesting . . . once my parents told me, like everything made sense. Like since I was very young like I would always be like, oh, can we go to Mexico? Like I want to see my family, and they were like, no, we can't. Or, when you turn sixteen and you want to get a permit to work with your friends at the mall, like they told me I couldn't because my dad was like, oh, the minute you start working you start getting money and you think that's all you want to do so you can't work. So, I was like okay. And the same thing with driving. I would always ask them like, oh, can I start driving, because I can get my permit, and he was like, no, we are not going to pay insurance for you, it's going to be too high. So, there was always a reason behind what I couldn't do and I just was like, my parents are strict, like I am not going to fight that. So, it wasn't until after that I started to realize like, oh, okay, they were doing all of this because they knew what my situation was.

Said Gabriel, who first came to the U.S. when he was two years old, then went back to Mexico and returned to the U.S. when he was five, "I always knew there was something, it's kind of like when you are a little kid and they tell you, well, you weren't born here, and you don't have the same sort of stuff that other people do." Gabriel came back to the U.S. using a cousin's papers and was told that if anyone asked, that his uncle and aunt were his dad and mom.

The majority of the students attended elementary, middle, and high school in the U.S. All but two students attended public high schools, some with large proportions of undocumented students; others felt that they were the only ones who were undocumented in their whole school.

Getting into College

All of the students found the college admissions process challenging. On top of their first generation college status, they were unsure whether or when to reveal their unauthorized status. As most Jesuit universities use the Common Application, which includes questions about citizenship and a request for a social security number, the presence of such questions (even though optional at most schools) intimidated students. This lack of knowledge about what was required for admission and uncertainty about whether they could safely ask questions about how to fill out the form created a dilemma for students, as indicated by Sandra: "It was a bit scary because once you start filling out the application and the first thing they ask you for is a social security number, it's extremely intimidating because how can you leave that part blank?"

The college admissions process for undocumented students was primarily navigated through informal networks. Undocumented students relied on a wide variety of sources to obtain information about how to apply and then later how to make it through college. Some had knowledgeable high school admissions counselors who served as very important sources of support and encouragement to apply to college. They also were information brokers between the students and the universities to which they applied. Counselors and teachers in this role called the university admissions office and asked questions about how students should fill out the admissions applications without social security numbers and if there were possibilities for financial aid. These actions by counselors allowed the students to remain anonymous and to feel more confident and honest in the application process.

However, getting this help was not always easy. Some students stated that they had to "come out" as undocumented to their high school teachers and counselors when being questioned about why they were not applying to high-ranking colleges. A few students said they had to "train" some of these advocates who said they had never worked with an undocumented student before and had no idea if they could go to college or not. However, some of these counselors became some of the strongest advocates for students, calling universities and asking questions on their behalf, and promoting the students' cases, especially to financial aid officers. Some students formed very close bonds with their high school counselors or teachers through this process of revealing their situation and receiving support that resulted in the opportunity to attend college, a goal that they worried they could never accomplish because of their status and lack of financial resources. Talking about a counselor at high school, Reina shared, "Our relationship was more than student-counselor . . . . when I got the scholarship I ran to her office and the entire office knew because I had been faxing papers for months right? So it was kind of like this celebratory moment. It was the most amazing thing. So, I mean, she cried. It was just, it was really powerful."

As indicated by Patricia, encouraging teachers and counselors made a huge difference in students' lives and their ability to go to college, "I had really encouraging counselors and teachers, and they really supported me, like they paid for my application fees, and they would drive me places, so . . . I still keep in touch with them, and I give workshops at the high school. I think that undocumented students need to have those mentors because you won't go anywhere without the mentors. A documented person needs mentors too, but it's really key for undocumented students to have them because you need that strong network and support."

When applying to a scholarship program offered through a nonprofit organization, Sandra talked about the reaction when she hesitantly told the executive director of the organization of her status: "She was surprised because she said that she never really knew of this situation. She really took the time to listen to me because a lot of people just have this stereotype of immigrants being bad and things of those sort. I was very grateful because after that I thought she wasn't going to like me anymore."

Only one student had the experience of reaching out and then being told that he couldn't go to a four-year school. Raul shared, "I talked to my guidance counselor, and when I told her that I was undocumented and I wanted to see if there was a way I could go to college at least, she said no.

She said that there is no way to go to college. Forget about it. There is no way because of my status . . . So that really brought me down. And from that point I did not talk to any guidance counselors; I just did everything through the people I knew through my pastor."

Other students either didn't think anyone could help them and did not talk to anyone in their high schools about their status, or when they did, their questions were met with uncertainty. Students who received no support from teachers or high school advisors talked to other students "in my situation" who had graduated, or with whom they were currently in high school. In two cases, students had older siblings who were also undocumented, who told them how to fill out their applications and about scholarships and people to talk to in the university admissions offices.

A few students, including Irma, noted that when they called college admissions offices to ask questions about financial support for undocumented students or admissions they encountered people who did not know what undocumented meant. "I had quite an experience at [one Jesuit University], I was receiving information that they wanted me to apply and that they would even waive my fee for the application, and I had a couple of questions about my status, and I called them and they were a little rude. The person I talked to, they basically did not know what an undocumented student was, and they told me, well, if you are not a citizen, then why are you even going to a university?" The student did not apply there, but applied to another Jesuit university she identified as "welcoming." In at least three cases students were asked by some of the schools to which they applied to fill out international student forms as part of the application process. Students were confused and sometimes scared by this request and did not follow through applying to those schools when that occurred. Uncertainty about how to navigate the process along with questions about what their lack of legal status meant for them in the future added to the typical stress of applying to college that most students experience. Said Mara about her last year of high school, "It was just up and down. It was an emotional journey my senior year."

Once students figured out the application process, most students applied to many schools, both public and private, and got into most of them. The larger hurdle to overcome was financial. Most who were able to apply to public colleges were told they would have to pay out-of-state tuition, and they were not eligible for federal or state aid. As a result, students relied mostly on merit-based scholarships to pay for college. Students applied for many, many private scholarships, sometimes unsure whether they were eligible or not. Some made it through multiple rounds of interviews, finding out at the end that they had not received the scholarship, and unsure if their status was the reason. When receiving scholarships, especially those that paid full tuition as well as room and board, students were ecstatic, not believing their luck, but they also felt guilty, knowing that some of their friends or others they had met at the interviews for the scholarships were just as worthy as them, but could not ultimately go to college because of a lack of money. As Javier says: "The interviews [for the scholarship for undocumented students] were pretty intense, because you are there in the room with like everybody that is applying for the same scholarship and you know just a limited amount of people are going to get it. So it felt really competitive and intense, because you saw all the people you thought maybe they deserved it more than you did . . . there was so much to lose, you have your future, it's right there. There is nothing you can do about your situation." Students also worried that once they were in college, other students who had taken out large loans to attend would resent them if they found out about their status combined with their scholarships.

Many students described very surreal experiences of finding out they had received scholarships that would allow them to attend a four-year college and then the disbelief of their families. When told he received a scholarship with full tuition, room, and board, Gabriel said he was ecstatic but unsure how to feel and that, "my dad was like, 'you're undocumented, how can you get a scholarship?'" One student's mom thought that the whole scholarship process must be a scam. However, even with full or partial scholarships, undocumented students still struggled financially, with even modest costs such as food and books presenting additional financial strain.

Staying In

Financial

All of the students except one had families with limited finances. The struggle for students while in college was especially noticeable for students who did not receive full scholarships. "I always have a hold on my account [at school]" because of financial reasons. Students coped with this by borrowing books and if they had access to a job that didn't require papers, working up to thirty hours a week, mainly on the weekends in restaurants and babysitting or tutoring during the week. Commuter students often worked with their parents, helping to clean houses or do landscaping.

Some students also needed to financially contribute to their families, so they sacrificed buying books or eating on campus so they could help. Reina gave every other paycheck to her family. The threat of eviction and financial hardship was something that hung over the heads of students' families as well. One student talked about finding all the free events with food on campus as her main way of eating, because her mom was laid off from her job and had little money to help her with grocery money.

Students also felt guilty for not contributing enough to alleviate their family's financial hardships, as Gabriel shared: "And sometimes it's kind of like you feel guilty for not, you might have twenty extra dollars, and you might want to save those, but at the same time your family is, you know? But the way I think about it is like, well, I am in school right now, I am trying to survive, trying to not ask that much from them, so when it's my time to help them out I will help them out." This student also talked about his scholarship covering the cost of his on-campus health insurance, as he did not previously have insurance. Four students explained that their families were contributing in some form to pay for their tuitions. One explained that his mom tried to send money when she could but he tried really hard to not need her money, knowing she did not have extra.

Two of the six universities had merit and need-based scholarships for students who were undocumented that covered full tuition, room, and board. These scholarships often also allowed students to use the money toward books, laundry, and other campus expenses. Other campuses gave partial scholarships and, not having access to state, federal, or many private loans, students and their families struggled to pay the rest. These students commuted to save money and worked a variety of jobs to make up for what was not covered by their scholarships.

Six students spoke of finding other ways to make money on campus outside of the traditional payroll jobs. Two students mentioned a research mentorship program where they received a small stipend and whatever was necessary for their research including materials, books, and sometimes conference expenses. One of these students also spoke of participating in surveys in the Psychology department where he received gift cards for his participation, another received gift cards for being a research assistant. For one student, there were opportunities at the Jesuit office to make money working for special occasions. Finally, two students mentioned being an Orientation Leader and other activities where all students received a stipend rather than being placed on payroll. At some campuses students could work in the residence halls in exchange for room and board, but other campuses paid a small salary for such work and thus students who were undocumented were not eligible for those positions.

Transportation

For students who commuted (most of the students except for those who received a full scholarship that covered room and board), transportation to school every day was a major form of stress. Because students were not able to legally get a driver's license, they relied on family or friends to take them to and from college, or they drove without a license and feared getting pulled over. As Mara shared, "I drive here (school), so it's the constant fear of getting pulled over. It's always in the back of my mind like, 'oh my god, what if I get pulled over today or tomorrow or the next day?'"

Or if their parents drove them without a license, they worried that that was putting their parents at risk. One student's dad drove her to school, a forty-minute drive, and she took the two-hour bus ride home each day from school. Another student talked about the hardship her family experienced trying to afford bus passes for every member each month since no one could drive because of their statuses. Students also mentioned fear of traveling alone on the bus and walking home from the bus in neighborhoods that felt unsafe.

In some states parents had initially been able to get a driver's license without a social security number or birth certificate, but recent changes in laws meant that they were no longer able to renew their previously legal licenses. A few students traveled to states near where they were attending school, which did not require strict documentation of status, and obtained legal (although out-of-state) licenses. Although a few were fined when pulled over for not having an in-state license, they did not mind paying the fine and continuing to drive. But that was a strategy for only a few students we interviewed. Said Javier about it, "A lot of students try to go to another state and try to get a driver's license over there, but even that's really hard. I don't know anybody in (that state) that could help me out and I don't want to lie or anything like that and get in trouble for it."

Students living on campus, but without an identification card, could not fly, and thus took the bus long distances each time they went home. Some students had passports from the country in which they were born, and used that to fly.

Campus Climate and Culture Shock

Students experienced culture shock when first attending college because of the difference in demographics between the campus and their communities and high schools. "I come from a [high] school where over ninety-five percent of the students are Latino, so I was in culture shock for awhile," said Irma, and Mara stated, "It was strange to go to high school with majority Latinos and then in college being the only Latino in class."

Two students spoke of negative experiences with their roommates. One roommate made racist comments including that illegal immigrants should be deported. Said that student, "the culture shock aspect, no one told me about that part of college. It wasn't because I was undocumented, I encountered a lot of racism. My roommate was racist, we would get Cesar Chavez day off and she would be like 'why do we get this day off for a filthy Mexican?'" For another student the issue was documentation, and his roommate verbally attacked him when his roommate first realized he might be undocumented. Both spoke of the experiences with a tone of resiliency but were hesitant to share their status with others after these incidents.

Students also noted that there was a general difference in attitudes on campus from the communities in which they were raised, as Patricia indicated: "The way they (other students) talked and the things they talked about were a lot different from what I was used to talking about and, I mean, it was just different . . . I'm a Political Science major and we talked about immigration policy and there were a lot of students in the class who were like, 'oh we should just deport them all, there should be someone there just to shoot them.' I'd never been in a situation where they were talking about me in that way, because from the community that I come from, everyone is very aware of the issues and they wouldn't say anything like that." Ivan was hurt when a close friend started making jokes about immigrants, saying, "So we kind of got really heated in this situation where I was just like, I can't believe you said that. It was just the initial shock of how he found out [I was undocumented], because he was joking and I was like, 'that's not funny. You don't know who is around you; you don't know who you are offending, saying stuff like that.' And then I guess he put two and two together."

Sofia mentioned that such attitudes also existed with faculty, "Even with some professors, I don't know, sometimes I feel like it's like they have never seen a Hispanic person with an accent before. You get a different . . . . it just feels weird sometimes." When this happened she reminded herself that she worked hard and got into the university just like everybody else.

Of the twenty-five students interviewed, six described specific negative experiences they had on campus regarding their status. Again, students explained experiences with a variety of people including other students, professors, and staff members. Five students said that the lack of knowledge among faculty and staff was problematic and left them trying to figure things out on their own very frequently. One student wondered if staff at a public university might be more knowledgeable because there were more undocumented students on the campus, making it easier to talk to people. Three other students explained experiences with staff and faculty members including the Dean of Students, an advisor, and the Internship coordinator, who were unable to help them because of their status. A dean repeatedly told a student asking about how to deal with future major requirements for which he was ineligible, "We'll deal with that when we get there." Students felt this lack of knowledge was challenging for them, and they were frustrated with the responses of university staff.

There were limits in the types of conversations that students were comfortable engaging in on campus, particularly around issues of immigration. Although some students felt more comfortable sharing their status with the peers they trusted, they feared sharing it with university staff, either because of the potential legal repercussions for themselves or their families, concern that staff would disapprove of them in general, or because they found staff unhelpful or unable to provide assistance given their situation.

Support

Family support. Most students relied on their families and sometimes friends for emotional support; however, they noted that their family often did not understand or know how to help them with school-related concerns. Nine students explained that their main source of emotional support was family. Mothers, sisters, aunts, dads, and whole families were mentioned as a strong source of support. Some students spoke about calling and video-chatting with their families, while others lived at home and received constant support as they saw their families every day. Family was the most frequent response when students were asked about who they went to for support, most stating that their family is "always there" for them.

Peers. Beyond family, peers were the next main form of support and information for most students. Of the twenty-one students that responded concerning peer support, all but one had positive remarks about receiving or giving support to and from their peers. More than half stated that their peers were their main source of emotional support. Oftentimes this emotional support came from other undocumented students who understood where they were coming from and could share their experiences. Other times students mentioned roommates and friends that they became comfortable enough with to share their status even though they were not undocumented. Two students spoke of documented students reacting supportively upon hearing about their undocumented status. All of the students who spoke about emotional support from peers expressed some sense of trust and vulnerability with their peers with whom they could talk about the struggles of being undocumented. Peers who provided support often met each other through scholarship gatherings, groups, and events related to their status while others met randomly and eventually it came out that both were undocumented. Interacting with other undocumented students seemed to be extremely important to all of the students who spoke about receiving emotional support because they felt these friends really understood where they were coming from.

Sofia described the importance of having support from others in the same situation: "My friends who are also in that same situation, just because, I don't know, like I am a psychology major, so I am totally in support of like [off-campus programs] and stuff, but it's really hard to go there when I feel maybe they are not used to, or trained to know how to deal with it. And because of all of my friends, we are all very, like resilient, we are all about okay, we need to go to school and we need to do this, because this is our situation, but yeah, that's . . . I've usually been able to deal with it, but like sometimes if I'm like told, oh you can't participate in this, or you are not getting this, it gets really difficult and it's like, we just, among our friends, we are kind of our social support." Ari mentioned the need to connect with peers in the same situation to get ideas about what to do in the future: "I would tell them to continue and to ask other friends who have been in the same situation—to look up to people, to kids that they know that have graduated from their high school or other high schools around them that are undocumented and are going to school. To search for them and ask them what they've done."

Seven of the students spoke specifically about the experience of sharing their status with peers. Some students were very open and told peers soon after meeting them, especially in situations where they already knew others were undocumented such as in programs for first-generation college students or a club organized around the DREAM Act. Others told peers when they were confronted with challenges. For example, one student was not able to attend a school-sponsored trip to Mexico because of his status and explained that he did not know what to do, ended up sharing with a friend, and then found out that friend was also undocumented. One student spoke of a friend blatantly asking and being caught off guard, but later feeling comforted knowing that the friend knew. Few students described situations with peers where they disclosed their status and had a negative response; rather, students felt greater trust and understanding with friends once they were aware of their status.

Five students explained that they found out about important resources specifically for undocumented students from their peers. Two explained that they found out about their universities from undocumented students who had attended their high schools and through them realized that they could go to college. Others found out about scholarships, clubs, and other support systems on campus from their undocumented peers. Reina described this support as, "It's like a community, you know, you find out information, how to get a job, how to do this, how to do that, and you kind of just exchange it, because it's so underground, like information." Four students described receiving academic support from their peers. Students spoke of their peers helping them to choose classes, giving them information about specific professors and helping them with classes that they had taken. Academic support was much less frequently mentioned compared to emotional support, and it seemed that academic support came more from teachers and advisors. Still, some of the students felt their peers were an important support academically.

Four students specifically mentioned the importance of getting advice as well as a desire to help other undocumented students. Sergio said the advice he would give is, "Simply that [going to college] is possible because a lot of students don't even consider it. Right away they begin to work and don't continue their education because they don't see why they should go." Two others spoke of the importance of knowing that others are ahead of you completing college and finding jobs; they explained the importance of finding these people and felt that they could be that type of support for others.

Four students reported that they did not have much outside emotional support but rather were their own main sources of support. These students either felt that they were not close enough or did not trust others or just did not have others in their life that understood their situation. Feelings of disappointment and pride were mixed strategies of internal support for these students. One student explained that she ran and drew when she needed emotional support, habits she started in high school to lower her stress level after experiencing depression related to finding out about her status.

Campus support. In terms of support on campus, of the twenty-five students interviewed, nine spoke specifically of positive experiences where they received support from a variety of people on campus. Students talked of teachers, advisors, retreat leaders, Jesuits, and other students all as people from whom they had found support, both academic and emotional. Professors were most frequently mentioned as a source of academic support while retreat leaders, Jesuits, and staff connected to scholarships or programs were more frequently turned to for emotional support. Students spoke of positive experiences both in relation to and completely separate from their undocumented status.

Patricia found two faculty members who were very supportive: "I came out to her [Psychology professor] and told her I was undocumented and she was like, 'oh, we are going to help you in whatever way we can,' and she helps me also when I am feeling really stressed out . . . and [another professor], he's been really encouraging and supportive and just never gives up on trying to help you. If you need something, like, I needed a binder and he got it for me, just things like that." At one campus, the admissions officer who helped Gabriel when he first applied continued to be the source of support during his whole time in college.

Two students explained that they had become more comfortable sharing their status, but were still very selective about whom they told. Teresa explained that she told "mostly people who I think could benefit from knowing that. So, like, I mentioned last week I did a program here on campus for high school students who are looking at going to college, but a lot of them have that same issue and don't know how to do it. So I'm . . . I like, I am completely open to certain people, like even if I don't know them, I will tell them, you know, this is what it's like, and it's rough, but you can do it." The theme of how and if to tell people differed among the respondents but was something that students thought about a lot.

For some students, the Catholic affiliation of the institution helped them feel more supported. Carlos shared, "I feel like this school, maybe because of the Jesuits, and our motto, and what we stand for, we're more like, we're more helpful, and we're more understanding of what's going on, whereas just reading somebody based on their paperwork." Similarly, Raul shared, "I am a religious person myself, so that's why I applied here too . . . I also feel happy here because it's a religious school, and I like that, it's important."

Groups on campus. For some students, groups for certain scholarships or first-generation college students served as sources of support and a means to meet their friends who ultimately became very important sources of support. The students spoke of finding others in their situation through sharing their stories in structured spaces or simply becoming more comfortable to share over time.

Students at a college that had a program that gave about five scholarships a year to students who were undocumented said that the program provided a means to connect with other students and was a support network to talk about challenges, frustrations, and options for the future. One student said that she was not part of a first-generation program at her university for undocumented students because she was unaware of her citizenship status when she applied to college. Once she better understood her status the student sought out other students who were also undocumented and then was made aware of many more resources, including access to help from an on-campus lawyer. But some students were wary of being associated with other students who were undocumented, or cautious about keeping the status of others confidential, stating, "We try not to spread it outside, like not say, Oh, we're undocumented or something like that. And we really respect that, because we are not all feeling the same way. Some people feel more comfortable publicly saying, I am undocumented, and you know, that's great, and there's a lot of us who respect it, that don't want to just tell everybody, but at least within ourselves we know, we kind of like give support to each other."

Being in College

On Campus Involvement

Students mentioned the inability to participate in many activities on campus because of their status. These activities mirrored the limitations in participation also brought up in the interviews conducted with staff. The activities most mentioned included travel abroad (for study and/or alternative break trips), work on campus, and campus leadership positions such as Resident Assistant and student government when pay was involved. Students also mentioned limitations in participating in research, attending academic conferences, certification to be an Emergency Medical Technician on campus, and completing internships required of their majors, especially if government funding supported the activity. Many students participated in programs and opportunities for which other students received stipends, but because students we interviewed could not get paid, but wanted the experience, they convinced university personnel to let them "volunteer." At one campus, a faculty member raised money from other faculty to pay students who were undocumented for research positions that the university provided as paid positions for documented students.

Students in majors that oriented them toward careers in healthcare, social work, engineering, accounting, and teaching attempted to get internships and find out about requirements for certification, and talked about being blocked because of a lack of a social security number. University staff were unable to help students around such barriers. Some students changed their majors, realizing that they would not be able to complete the requirements embedded in the major or work in that field after graduation. Others waited, hoping something would change by the time they reached that part of their degree program or graduated. While some students were practical in choosing fields most likely to orient them toward graduate or professional school and delay dilemmas about how to obtain professional jobs, other students were passionate about the fields they wanted to pursue and kept doing so, even if they thought it would work against them later. Like Reina shared, "I think that there is a huge pressure for a lot of undocumented students to do something that will get you a job. I think kind of ignoring your passions, a lot of the time. I think that I am going to end up choosing something that will help, whether that's Sociology for the community organizing kind of understanding, social structures and doing community organizing kind of just something like that. I am very passionate about politics and community organizing, so I feel like that is probably going to end up being what I end up doing, regardless of what people kind of say, like, well, you have a scholarship, do something practical, or whatever. But I feel like there is never a right answer and there is never something practical you can do, because regardless of what you major in, it is going to be difficult to get a job. So, you might as well do something that you are passionate about while you have this funding."

Travel as a major barrier to participation in activities. Many students said that if they heard that travel or pay would be involved in a co-curricular activity they were interested in, they did not even try to apply. For example, Juan Carlos shared, "Model UN, I have hesitated going to most meetings and actually becoming a really active member because I know that they take trips outside of the country and I don't want to be in that position to explain or have an excuse every time, so if I actually take a really active role, and I know that they participate in competitions, so if I become a good candidate for the competitions, I am going to have to explain, come up with some kind of an excuse as to why I couldn't go. So it's kind of a sticky situation for that, and I hesitate participating in some of those . . . Yeah. And the service trips are something that I really, really want to do, and I was even considering going to either New York, New York wouldn't be too bad, but I wanted to be able to go to New Orleans, and it's always a risk to leave the place, to leave [this state] and get on a plane, it's always a risk. So I kind of hesitated doing it."

Said Ivan, "I would have loved to have studied abroad or alternative spring breaks. My friend just got back from El Salvador doing work with Engineers without Borders and I was like, that's so cool! Not only did you embrace another culture, you are coming back and helping them out, and I wish I could be a part of that kind of change." Not being able to participate as well as having to come up with an explanation for why they were not going bothered students, as Carlos stated: "People are asking 'how come you never go abroad, why don't you take advantage of your resources?' It hurts."

Sandra expressed not only hesitation but fear related to participating in activities that required travel: "I don't know I just kind of feel I have this trauma that I can't do these things because I'm afraid something is going to happen." Missing out on things that other students were able to do and they could not took an emotional toll, as Sergio shared: "I always knew that I didn't have papers, but I never knew that I would be missing out on so much, especially to go to college."

Limitations in staff being able to help. A few students, like Sergio, tried to be more involved in co-curricular activities, but became disappointed when university staff could not help them figure out if they could participate or not:

> Well sometimes when they have meetings/presentations with various companies for internships—I can go but it's almost impossible for them to give me an internship. The majority of them ask for a social security number so it's not that they prohibit me, but almost because of the social security number requirement. That has been a challenge for me. I've emailed [internship staff coordinator] about it. I could tell she wanted to help, but at the same time, they're very misinformed so it was like, "oh, you look on your own." I was getting a few emails about

internship fairs and I emailed her: "I don't have a social security number, what can I do? Could I enter through the school, as a student so they wouldn't have to ask for my social?" First she sent me a message saying, "Let me research and I'll give you a response within a week." And then she responded "I couldn't find much information but I encourage you to apply." I mean, my mom could tell me that, "work hard." So it was kind of like, "You apply by your own means."

Inequity in participation. As stated earlier, some students "volunteered" for positions for which they knew that other students were paid. But some opportunities that had to be paid in some way did not have even this as an option. As mentioned, on some campuses students can apply to be a resident assistant in the residence halls as it comes with free room and board, but at other schools the position is only available to students who qualify for work-study, and thus is not an option for students who are undocumented. This really frustrated Gabriel who wanted to have the leadership experience that the position brings: "We got to a school where it's all about social justice, but within the school we face these barriers. And what makes that person more valuable than I am?" Students who commuted said that this was their main barrier to participation in campus activities and did not link their lack of participation to their undocumented status.

Privacy, Secrecy, and Living a Dual Life

Students spoke of feeling very conflicted about their situations and living the life of a carefree college student along with the realization that they were very different from their fellow classmates. The need to hide their status while growing up—not just for themselves, but also for their families—dominated their thoughts. The fear of parents is very real for Beatriz: "My parents, after they told me (of my status), they were like you can never tell anyone. This is very dangerous. You could put the family at risk"; and Sam said, "See, growing up with this situation, I really learned to be a private person. I keep everything to myself. Knowing that everything you have worked for could be taken away from you at any second, and I could be sent back at any second makes you really want to shut up about everything."

Telling can also be emotionally draining, as Mara, who used to share her story more but doesn't so as not to "break down" said, "I'm completely comfortable with saying to you or anyone else that I'm undocumented, but I don't want to go into my life story and I went through this. I feel like that's something I just deal with within myself."

Students who came to the United States as babies can't imagine living anywhere else and are fearful of all they know being taken away if their status is found out. Sam, who couldn't remember anything before being in the U.S., explained: "I don't remember anything else. I only remember being here. It terrifies me to know that that can be taken away from me. I just wish it wouldn't be."

A few students, like Reina, said they had learned from experience that "I don't come out to a lot of people." One student had a bad experience in high school that made him wary of telling college officials about his status, and he worried that once people knew they couldn't get past knowing that information to help him: "How do you get over this kind of stuff (own political/personal opinion) and counsel a student?" Marvin said that in college, "One professor that I had in class, he said something about 'I don't think immigrants should be getting scholarships' and stuff like that . . . so I'm not going to him with my problems." Comments such as this and the ignorance of documented students about immigration issues and how citizenship was granted caused many students to be very careful to hide their status, and even to be prepared with answers that did not reveal their statuses if asked why they were not working or studying abroad, and so on.

The two students who had had experiences with almost being deported were more open about their statuses, figuring that officials already knew them and it was now their responsibility to speak out for others who could not. But they were still selective. Said one of the students who was almost deported just before coming to college, "I'm open about it if people want to talk about it, but I don't go around shouting it on the mountain tops either."

Reactions to telling. When students did decide to reveal their status to college officials or friends, the reactions were often mixed and unpredictable. As mentioned earlier, more than one student described university staff and college friends as being "shocked" when they told them about their status.

Students also spoke of being tired of having to tell people everything about their histories, just to get some help for a current problem. Heidi shared, "It's a long story to tell. I tell people and they say, 'well, couldn't you just do this and that' and I'm like, 'no, no you can't' and they say they didn't know. So it's good to see that you are educating them in a way." When Beatriz finally told her research professor, the professor said, "I don't know what to do." Said Beatriz, "If he doesn't know what to do, how am I supposed to know what to do?"

Many students, like Ari, feared the reactions of their friends: "I think they wouldn't respect me. I feel like if they knew that I didn't have papers they would probably say 'what a waste of a student. Another student could be in her place with this scholarship taking the classes.' That's how I feel." This led to isolation for some students, as Sofia stated: "I am not really open about my situation. Like even with my friends, I don't say anything about my situation, so I like to just keep it to myself, so that's why I don't talk to people." Charlie also shared, "My parents would always tell me that I shouldn't tell people, that something could happen, you never know like they are going to turn against you." The same student talked about finding out a year after he met one of his good friends, that the friend was undocumented as well, which felt like a relief.

As in high school, some students had good experiences with people after revealing their status. Ivan "took a chance" which resulted in a scholarship for $10,000 in cash he could use for books which was a "huge help." He indicated, "You kind of learn to pick up who you can and cannot trust. Even within my friends."

Living a dual life. Students talked about what it felt like to be living a dual life, on the one hand a dream life of being a full-time college student with no cares in the world, and then the life of an undocumented person who could be found out and whose life could change dramatically any minute, as Reina shared: "It's like you live kind of a dual life, like you are a student and you are responsible for keeping this high GPA to maintain your scholarship, which is kind of your anchor, your life support, emotional to your family, it can also be financial support to your family, and you also kind of have to look out for yourself in a lot of different ways. It's like I'm doing my club stuff or I'm riding my bike around campus going to class, whatever, having a great time laughing and getting coffee with friends, and then you go to your room, close the door, and then your lawyer calls you . . . And it's just kind of a strange kind of binary to be in, like you are in a very, you are tied to your legal status, but you are also free." Javier noted, "I wish I could always be a student and not have to worry about, after your four years, you are done. I wish this could last a little longer, because it keeps your mind off of being . . ." As a result of being in this situation, students saw some of their friends who were undocumented become depressed during their last year of college.

Encounters with law officials and legal problems while a student also exacerbated students' feelings of living a dual life. For some students this happened even before they started college: When coming to visit the college after being accepted, Gabriel flew using his school identification card which was not accepted by the airport and he was pulled aside, "and all I could think about was losing my scholarship and having to go back to Mexico . . . I was really traumatized by that," so now he takes the bus.

Another student and a sibling were arrested for not having proper papers when traveling on the train from their college to visit a friend at another college during spring break. Said Sandra, "It's a daily worry [deportation] because I don't know if today might be my last day. I don't know if I'm coming back home. Even driving—we even fear getting pulled over by the cops because we have heard of them asking for your status. We're more apt to being asked because we look Hispanic. It's a struggle every day. We [family members] just go out for the necessary things."

While it was tempting to just forget one's status in the college context, Patricia encouraged students to never forget their status while also savoring the college experience, "Just not isolating yourself, because sometimes it's easier just to isolate yourself. Especially here [at college] because you have all the resources, you can forget sometimes that you are undocumented. And it's essential for someone not to forget that, and to always try to build those relationships with faculty and staff too, because they can help you, start early, in freshman year." Said Mara about being in college, "I'm enjoying this while it lasts. Like I said, it's my little bubble. I'm going to college and it's free. But I know that a lot of people don't get this opportunity, that's why I'm grateful."

Students wanted to live in and fully appreciate the experience of having the opportunity to go to college. They expressed gratitude and the realization that being able to be in college was a "dream come true," something they and their parents never thought could actually happen.

Carlos shared, "To me it's a privilege and an honor to be in college." From Sam, "I'm so grateful to the college for helping me . . . I couldn't be more grateful."

Moving On

In some ways, asking students about their future plans was the most stressful part of the interviews for students. Students were extremely uncertain about their futures; Fabiola was hopeful, but very uncertain: "But I know that after I graduate from here, it's like, what am I going to do next? It's hard because . . . I don't know . . . Sometimes I'm discouraged, too, like, oh, why am I doing this [going to college]?" Students mentioned many fears about facing their post-graduation lives and each student experienced it differently. The fears ranged from emotional stress to increased family pressure and uncertainty about confronting their legal status as an adult.

Employment

Overall the greatest barrier facing students after graduation was employment. Many discussed feeling trapped, having spent so much time studying only to return home to jobs like babysitting, working in restaurants, and cleaning. With many doubting their ability to get jobs in their fields, similar to students facing a challenging job market, almost all of the students we interviewed strongly considered going to graduate school, but worried about how they could afford it. Teresa, for example, stated, "So, I'm like, well, hopefully when I'm getting my PhD, like, things turn around. At the same time that there is a lot of frustration, there is also a lot of hope. So, it's just about kind of finding those people. You know? Who are in your boat and who are able to just guide you, you know? Through the process. And, just waiting."

Students' career choices were heavily influenced by their immigration status. While they expressed interest in careers such as teaching, accounting, engineering, and health or in being involved with internships or on-campus leadership, they realized that those choices required some sort of identity verification that they were unable to apply for because of their status.

Students like Irma also heard stories of immigration status blocking career choices for students who graduated before them: "I heard of an accounting major who was also undocumented, and I think she was working at a fast food restaurant after she graduated. She couldn't get her CPA (license) because she couldn't take the test as it required a social security number." Students had specific questions about whether they should go on interviews or reveal their status on job interviews. Career Center staff were not helpful to students in regards to these questions. So students worried about if or when they should tell others. A number of students mentioned hoping that the DREAM Act would eventually pass, thus changing their employment prospects.

Emotional Stress

Dealing with emotional stress around current and future plans was a constant issue for students. Sandra shared, "Sometimes it really depresses me a lot because I feel like I'm not valued as an individual because of that—like I'm not worth as much as everyone else because of this. I can't do this because of that or I'm not deserving so it makes me feel depressed because I want to do stuff that everyone else is doing, and I can't . . . I'm pretty much stuck just waiting for my chance, waiting for my opportunity."

Sofia said, "I feel like I'm working so hard and I feel like sometimes it's just going to be for nothing. Even though I know that's not true, but sometimes I do think that way. Because you know, I see all the things happening right now and it's like the thing in Arizona [referring to anti-immigration laws], things like that that makes me feel scared and worried because I don't know what's coming . . . . So I feel sad every day."

Legal Status

Most students' prospects for legal status in the United States under laws at the time of the interviews were dim. Only one student was on a path to citizenship. Most of the students had talked to lawyers at some point, and were told that they had no path to citizenship, unless maybe another member of their family could sponsor them if they themselves first received citizenship. A few students, like Javier, reflected on the fact that once they turned 18 or 21, they were "on their own."

Because most students had lived so many years in the United States without authorization, their chances for citizenship through sponsorship without leaving the U.S. were unlikely. Those who were in relationships and considered marriage to a citizen were told by lawyers that they would have to return to their home countries for a number of years and apply for sponsorship after the period of time was over. Two students had citizen children and said that leaving was not an option for them.

One student, Irma, mentioned the example of her brother, who was also undocumented and went to college in Mexico, but now that he left could not come back to the U.S. In wondering if she would ever see him again, Irma also reflected on what the experience was like for him and by extension what it could be like if she also went that route: "It's kind of a weird experience [for him, being in Mexico], because it's his native country, but he's more of an American, so it's weird because there is a saying in Spanish that you are not from there, but you are not from here, so you are stuck in between . . . He does have those privileges of being able to drive around and not be worried about being asked for his license or anything, but then again, he misses everything."

Student Suggestions for Institutions

Students had many suggestions about what colleges could do to improve the experiences for students who were undocumented. The suggestions ranged from help for students during the application process, to improving experiences on campus, and helping with issues related to career development pre- and post-graduation.

First, students wanted campuses that accepted and provided funding for students who were undocumented to better advertise their openness to applicants, as Reina suggested: "It's hidden, you know. I am sure there are many students going to school not having all their legal documents." The combined data from students and staff revealed the importance of social capital and the very informal and ad hoc nature of the admissions process for undocumented students, many of whom made it to college only because of the luck of speaking to the "right" person in the admissions office or knowing people who had already navigated the admissions system at that school and could refer them to specific people for help, or having an assertive and persistent high school advisor or teacher.

Once on campus, students wanted an advocate they could go to who understood their story and could help them with a variety of issues, including navigating the system and processes, so that they would not have to tell their stories over and over again to different people. Students experienced a long process of trying to figure out, on their own, whom they could trust to tell their stories, and then hoping that it would be worth it in the end because the person actually had the ability to help them. So students wanted one person or one office on campus to go to for any questions they had that involved their undocumented status. Most campuses are not set up to provide such support, with people knowledgeable about all the different departments and programs. In one case, the admissions officer who helped undocumented students during the application process became their go-to person on campus. Presumably this was not in that person's job description.

In the absence of one person who was trained to help students, students suggested more training for university staff so they would be more informed when students discussed their situations. Students hoped that such training might reduce the likelihood of students encountering blank stares or comments such as "I've never heard of that before" or "I am not sure."

Similarly, for academic help, students like Beatriz said things such as, "If there was a way to know which professors to go talk to, like which professors we would feel comfortable going up to . . . people always say, go to your professors, go to their office hours, talk to them, get to know them, and that's really difficult when you don't want to share that part of your life." One student, who helped start a club for students who were undocumented on campus, said that there was conversation on campus about providing stickers that could be put on faculty and staff offices to signal that the person was comfortable and knowledgeable about the issues and was safe to talk to and ask for help as well as put together a list of faculty and staff allies that students could go to.

One college had a lunch for all undocumented students the first semester so students could meet each other, and this became an important support group during their time at the college. One student mentioned that having lunch each semester with his advisor who knew his situation was helpful, and another student talked about how much she appreciated the quarterly talks with the Jesuit in charge of the scholarship program who provided both tangible, instrumental, as well as emotional support.

Many students, such as Ivan, commented on how important it was for students to reach out and ask for help. "It just takes some courage and being brave." The need for encouragement was also mentioned by students like Marvin: "I would have liked for somebody to tell me to not be afraid, like don't see this as some kind of barrier. You could still do what you want to do. It's going to be harder, you're going to have to work harder, but you can eventually get to where you want to be."

Because financial stressors were such an everyday part of college, and students wanted to be more involved in campus life, students hoped for creative ways that they could be involved on campus in positions for which they could receive pay. Some campuses appeared to have figured out ways to legally provide assistance through setting up their scholarships in ways that allowed students to pay for their books and other daily needs.

Of course, students also wanted assistance being able to obtain internships off campus, as stated by Juan Carlos: "I don't know if it's possible, but to have a partnership with a company where I could work as part of the university so they wouldn't have to ask for my social. Simply that as a [partner university] student, with good grades, and will do good work instead of concentrating on the fact that I don't have papers. I don't know; an association with a company [names company] who I know helps in a lot of that. They'd be supporting their students and allowing us to enter the workforce, even without a social security number." Some students also said that access to a lawyer while a student to better understand their undocumented status and potential legal work opportunities would be helpful.

And although some students did not want to think about graduation and the next step, many students had suggestions related to how others could help them with the question of what to do post-graduation. Nico suggested help getting connected to a network of people who have already navigated after college issues (graduate school, financial aid, applying for jobs, post-college service, and so on): "I would like a little guidance. Maybe like, knowing my options would be really good. It's sort of a gray area right there, I don't know what's going to happen after these four years."

Conclusion

Overall, we found that both institutionally and for students, informality was peppered throughout students' experiences and the ways that most campuses responded to the presence of students who were undocumented in their admissions process and existence on their campuses. The consequence of this wide array of informal procedures is inconsistency and a lingering perception among undocumented students that they are not fully supported at Jesuit institutions.

Students provided several recommendations on how colleges can better support those with undocumented status, including advertising funding opportunities, creating opportunities for deeper awareness of the issues at the staff level—from the admissions office to professors—providing support in obtaining internships and work experience, and providing on-campus advocates for undocumented students to approach comfortably. Despite the many challenges that students faced in being in college, including a hostile climate in some cases and financial barriers, students thrived and did well academically. Colleges that are able to assist these high-achieving and determined students will be able to play an important part in fulfilling their missions. However, for students to fully realize their potentials, especially after graduation, federal laws and policies will need to change.

Notes

1. Leisy Janet Abrego, "'I Can't Go to College Because I Don't Have Papers': Incorporation Patterns of Latino Undocumented Youth," *Latino Studies* 4 (2006): 212–231. Roberto G. Gonzales, "Learning to Be Illegal: Undocumented Youth and Shifting Legal Contexts in the Transition to Adulthood," *American Sociological Review* 76 (2011): 602–619.

2. Rubén G. Rumbaut and Golnaz Komaie, "Immigration and Adult Transitions," *The Future of Children* 20 (2010): 43–66.

3. Tanya Golash-Boza, *Immigration Nation: Raids, Detentions, and Deportations in Post-9/11 America* (London, UK: Paradigm Publishers, 2012). Anna Sampaio, *Terrorizing Latina/o Immigrants: Race, Gender, and Immigration Politics in the Age of Security* (Philadelphia, Pa.: Temple University Press, 2015).

4. Lesley Bartlett and Ofelia Garciá, *Additive Schooling in Subtractive Times: Bilingual Education and Dominican Immigrant Youth in the Heights.* Stacey J. Lee, *Up Against Whiteness: Race, School, and Immigrant Youth* (New York: Teachers

College Press, 2005). Mariá Pabón López and Gerardo R. López, *Persistent Inequality: Contemporary Realities in the Education of Undocumented Latina/o Students* (New York: Routledge, 2010).

5. Gonzales, "Learning to Be Illegal."

6   From Research to Action

*Jesuit Institutional Practices in Response
to Undocumented Students*

SUZANNA KLAF AND KATHERINE
KAUFKA WALTS

Overview

Jesuit colleges and universities share a common mission—to educate "the whole person," to foster inclusive communities of excellence, and to promote social justice; however, the institutional policies, capacities of staff, and responses to undocumented students vary across the twenty-eight Jesuit colleges and universities in the United States, and members of the U.S.-based Association of Jesuit Colleges and Universities (AJCU). It is within these varying contexts that we explore the insights and experiences of staff in working with undocumented students, as well as the actions taken by staff to uphold the Jesuit mission.

This chapter explores institutional responses to undocumented undergraduate students from the perspective of staff. Data from 110 key staff members (employed in admissions, financial aid, student services, campus ministry, and so on) from across all twenty-eight institutions were collected through an online survey, were analyzed, and are presented in this chapter. Additionally, the findings were enriched by information gathered from a series of in-depth interviews with staff collected from across six of the twenty-eight Jesuit colleges and universities (JCUs) in the U.S. Whereas interviewed undocumented students shared stories of the struggles of their families and stories of hope in accessing higher education, interviewed staff members provided an institutional narrative. Staff took pride in serving undocumented students, and found creative ways to address the wide range of student needs. Given their experiences and their understanding of undocumented student needs, the staff provided suggestions for the institutionalization of practices that could be useful for all types of public and private colleges and universities.

The first section of this chapter highlights the results of the survey and interviews conducted with JCU staff. In the second section, a five-part case study of Loyola University Chicago initiatives is presented. These initiatives were informed by the engagement of Loyola University Chicago in the research partnership, the results of which are presented in this chapter, and the dissemination of the Ford-funded report composed in collaboration with Fairfield University and Santa Clara University. Through strong leadership and collaboration between faculty, staff, and students, a concrete blueprint for taking action has been developed at Loyola and is shared here.

Methodology

The research informing the first section of this chapter was collected over two years (2010–2012) by research teams at Fairfield University in Connecticut, Santa Clara University in California, and Loyola University Chicago in Illinois. Employing a mixed-methods research model, the project administered an online survey to American Jesuit colleges and universities staff, and conducted in-depth structured interviews with key staff (see the Introduction to this book for an in-depth discussion of the methodology used for the full study).

The online survey was designed to explore the practices and attitudes of staff toward serving undocumented students at all twenty-eight Jesuit colleges and universities across the United States. Approximately 200 staff from admissions, financial aid, student services, and campus ministry were invited to participate in the online survey, and 110 responded. To enrich the survey data, in-depth structured interviews were conducted at six JCU campuses—including two schools in the eastern region, two in the Midwest, and two in the West.

The data collected shed light on staff awareness of undocumented students enrolled at Jesuit colleges and universities (JCUs) and various practices of admissions, enrollment, financial aid, and student support that meet undocumented student needs.

Findings from Research Study Conducted in 2010–2012

"Ad Hoc" Institutional Policies & Procedures

JCUs lack official policies regarding the enrollment and support of undocumented students. Of the 110 surveyed staff, 74 percent agreed or strongly agreed that support for undocumented students at their institution was more informal than formal (Online survey of JCU staff, 2010–2011). Only 9.4 percent indicated that their institution had an official or formal process to enroll undocumented students, 23 percent reported that their university had an informal process, and 45 percent were unsure whether a formal or informal process was in place to enroll undocumented students (Online survey of JCU staff, 2010–2011).

Undocumented & "Under the Radar" on Jesuit Campuses

A significant percentage of staff and faculty were "not sure" whether or not there were undocumented students on their campuses (30 percent overall). Awareness of undocumented students on JCU campuses was limited to a handful of professional staff who worked closely with this specific student population. Student services staff were most aware of the presence of undocumented students on their campus (15 percent reporting "not sure").

Interviewed staff mentioned meeting undocumented students "either through the grapevine" or through referral by admissions, enrollment services, or the financial aid office, as "the student contacts Admissions usually first" (JCU staff interview, 2011).

Of the 110 survey respondents, 8 participants were able to estimate when their institution began admitting undocumented students. Responses included from the time the institution opened its doors to the last twenty years, the 1990s, and the early 2000s. Geographic location of the JCU mattered with 96 percent of staff at Jesuit universities in the West indicating they had undocumented students versus 50 percent at universities in the East who were "not sure" (Online survey of JCU staff, 2010–2011).

Estimates of the number of undocumented students enrolled at JCUs are not readily available. Over three-quarters (or 77 percent) of staff could not provide a precise number of undocumented students on their campus. Professional staff were unaware of the presence of undocumented students in the application pool and those enrolled unless students disclose or provide incomplete paperwork (i.e., on questions requesting citizenship status or social security number) or self-disclose (Online survey of JCU staff, 2010–2011).

Students are not asked to reveal their status when they apply, and admission officers take a "don't ask—don't tell" approach (JCU staff comment, online survey, 2010–2011). Filing errors or omissions made by students are what tip University staff off to potential undocumented students, a method that according to a staff member "isn't foolproof" (JCU staff interview, 2011). Staff become aware of undocumented students when they leave application questions blank, a "potential red flag" according to one staff member (JCU staff interview, 2011). Interviewed staff mentioned that it is common for undocumented students to leave some application questions blank. These omissions may include social security number and citizenship status. Submitting a social security number is not required when applying for admission, though necessary for financial aid applications, and the same is true of citizenship status. A university becomes aware of a potentially undocumented student if he or she discloses or if his/her paperwork (e.g., FAFSA, financial aid) is not "in order" in which case the university would need to follow up with the student. However, self-identification of status as "other" is not problematic, as one staff mentioned "you could get away with leaving it as other" (JCU staff interview, 2011). Although 36 percent of surveyed staff indicated that there was an option for "other" on admission documents concerning citizenship status, 54 percent of survey respondents indicated that their admissions documents required students to note their citizenship status—whether on the Common Application or FAFSA (Online survey of JCU staff, 2010–2011). Verification of status is only done if the applicant is seeking financial aid. According to one admission staff, "we try to be really sensitive to not ask questions about . . . citizenship or country of origin [. . .] there's other ways to get the information without putting someone on the spot like that" (JCU staff interview, 2011).

Student "information is self-reported, so an undocumented student could very easily put on their application that they are a U.S. citizen [. . .] The financial aid system is really the only way to verify whether or not a student is a U.S citizen or eligible non-citizen" (JCU staff interview, 2011).

Some undocumented students apply as an "international" student. Two staff responsible for international students spoke to this point from their experience with undocumented students:

I know some of them inadvertently think they're international and they check off that box, and then when it comes to my attention and I probe a little bit, and then I've got to make some corrections, you know, because technically we still consider international to be the truly foreign students who are coming from overseas. (JCU staff interview, 2011)

Three staff mentioned that the citizenship status application question often clued them in to potential undocumented students:

. . . when students have answers which are either vague or say that they are a citizen of another country but don't give any sort of visa status, that's usually a clue as well that that student will need assistance as an undocumented student. (JCU staff interview, 2011)

A few schools flagged undocumented students in their records as "international students" for financial aid purposes or added a marker to distinguish their status.

Generally, no formal efforts were being made to track undocumented students in university records. Institutions collect "traditional" student records, all students are assigned an ID number, and "general data"/demographic information is collected. For instance, institutions identify first-generation students as mentioned by a staff member: "we don't look at undocumented students, we look at first generation but we know within that first generation there may be undocumented" (JCU staff interview, 2011). Additionally, those who become aware of undocumented students take precautions to not "keep [records] per their request" (JCU staff interview, 2011).

Three staff expressed concern over formal tracking practices, such as maintaining a database that identifies undocumented students out of concern of putting the students at risk:

I think that there's been a reluctance to put any sort of flag in their formal record because I don't think we want that stigma attached to students and I think there's always a concern that if federal policy changed at any point, I don't think we want to jeopardize those students in any way shape or form, probably selfishly we didn't want to jeopardize ourselves either. (JCU staff interview, 2011)

Given the challenge of accurately identifying undocumented students and the need to protect this vulnerable population, only 57.5 percent of surveyed staff knew of students at their institutions that would be considered undocumented, and 31.1 percent were not sure. They estimated that around 14 undocumented students had been enrolled at their institution since 2000. Fifty percent of the staff were not sure of how many accepted applicants at their institution may be undocumented, while 45.3 percent estimated that undocumented applicants made up less than two percent of the accepted pool (Online survey of JCU staff, 2010–2011).

With undocumented students representing such a small segment of the undergraduate student population at JCUs, it is a wonder how students know to apply. As the research finding showed, a network of internal and external actors proved essential in alerting undocumented students to opportunities at JCUs.

Undocumented Student Access to JCUs: Informal Networks and Procedures

Few JCUs were public about their welcoming undocumented applicants. Most undocumented students would find out about a JCU being accessible through "word of mouth," high school guidance counselor, admissions' visits to high schools, through friends, and their community parish / the Catholic network. These networks are crucial "as first generation children of immigrant parents" undocumented students are "not supported at home, there are language differences which often prevent the parents from getting involved in the college process, or just a lack of personal knowledge keeps them from getting involved" (JCU staff interview, 2011). Some students are "highly unaware of what they need to do" while some have advocates in the community that are assisting them (JCU staff interview, 2011).

EXTERNAL NETWORK OF ADVOCATES

Eighteen interviewed staff spoke about the informal external networks that bring undocumented students to their campuses. They reported that a variety of networks exist. In one case a staff member established a connection with a local parish where a priest acted as "gatekeeper" for undocumented students, guiding them to Jesuit institutions (JCU staff interview, 2011). The importance of the religious community network came up in three other interviews as well, with staff reporting the role of the "Jesuit network," "Jesuit feeder high school[s]," the "Cristo Rey Network," although local public schools and partnership programs also provided a pool of potential undocumented applications (JCU staff interview, 2011).

Five interviewed staff mentioned "third party" organizations that advocate for students by doing outreach to schools at the state and national levels, asking: "What are you doing with undocumented students?" and "What are your policies?" and "What can you do for these students?" (JCU staff interview, 2011). These organizations are working to identify colleges that provide financial assistance to undocumented students. Staff spoke of state-level discussions amongst university staff regarding what to do with undocumented students, as well as state coalitions that host events/ panels to inform undocumented students of higher education opportunities. The coalitions "come in and speak to the students and try to encourage them to follow through on their dreams and to find that one person at the institution that would advocate for them and help them get into the school" (JCU staff interview, 2011).

High school counselors aware of student status are able to help advocate for them and potentially alert admissions, while asking the difficult questions on behalf of undocumented students in what was described as a "cloak and dagger" way by one interviewee (JCU staff interview, 2011). For instance, a counselor might ask: "'Do you provide scholarships for international students without requiring them to apply for financial aid?' and oftentimes that was a way for folks to try to determine whether you would be able to assist an undocumented student" (JCU staff interview, 2011).

Six interviewed staff indicated that they work closely with high school guidance counselors, focusing on developing the relationship between the admissions staff and the applicant, thus establishing "long-standing deep relations." Counselors who have connections with admissions staff "will pick up the phone and say, 'I've got this hard luck case. What can you do for the student?'" Three other interviewed staff members spoke of being contacted by counselors:

A guidance counselor will give me a call and say, "[Name], I have this excellent student who's undocumented and is interested in [University], but what can we do for them?" or in some cases, "I have a student—not necessarily excellent—but who we are quite fond of and would like to be able to help them out somehow." (JCU staff interview, 2011)

Two interviewed staff spoke of high school teachers that advocate for undocumented students, acting as a "pipeline" and asking "can you help them out with their situation?" In one case, an Admissions counselor was aware of a high school teacher that was "very encouraging of students regardless of their immigration status" advocating for a number of undocumented students (JCU staff interview, 2011).

These external networks are essential for undocumented students in seeing Jesuit institutions as an option for accessing higher education, particularly as outreach efforts on the part of JCUs is rather limited.

RECRUITING UNDOCUMENTED STUDENTS

Sixty-five percent of surveyed staff indicated that there are no mechanisms in place to reach out to undocumented students interested in higher education; only 12.28 percent indicated that a few designated Admissions colleagues have experience working with underrepresented applicants (Online survey of JCU staff, 2010–2011).

Only 17 percent of staff respondents knowledgeable about admissions procedures reported that their institution had a mechanism for outreach to undocumented students. However, 55 percent indicated their institution had an informal program with high school guidance counselors regarding undocumented students (Online survey of JCU staff, 2010–2011). Of the 47 interviewed staff, there was mention that undocumented students are "recruited like any other student," "absent of the knowledge of whether they are documented or undocumented" (JCU staff comment, online survey, 2010–2011).

The undocumented student population overlaps with the high-achieving students that are recruited by JCUs, for instance first-generation students who may be sought out through the "Academic Talent Search," which encourages underrepresented populations of students to go to college. Often "urban students—first-generation students—many Latino or Latina students" are encouraged to apply (Online survey of JCU staff, 2010–2011).

At one institution, a staff member indicated a strong partnership with the Hispanic community, leading to efforts "to recruit Hispanic Americans" (JCU staff interview, 2011).

Although Jesuit institutions of higher education are welcoming to all high-achieving students, the active recruitment of undocumented students is not the norm. That is, most likely it is not on "anybody's radar" in the Admissions office (JCU staff interview, 2011). In fact, two interviewed staff members were uncertain but doubted their institution actively recruited undocumented students: ". . . only because I think we have limited resources, so we leave it open. Those students approach us, we definitely try to do what we can," and even if they did recruit, "I don't think that is something we would make very public" (JCU staff interview, 2011).

When Admissions Offices recruit students, they make choices of which communities to go to; however no intentional mention or explicit messaging is conveyed to actively recruit undocumented students. As one interviewed staff mentioned: "You're not going to go out and say 'hey, I want to sign up for as many undocumented students, that's my goal,' . . . you can make a decision to be in places that might be more likely to have students who were brought here by parents when they were toddlers and now are looking to go to college" (JCU staff interview, 2011).

At recruiting events the messaging to students is consistent with standard university practices, as one interviewed staff mentioned: "We tell students what we offer at the university, we explain financial aid packages, we mention if we don't get a social security number from you, you won't be able to fill out the FAFSA to be able to qualify. So the information, the process everything's there that's been there for years . . ." (JCU staff interview, 2011).

Recruiters committed to ensuring opportunities for all students to access higher education and knowledgeable of the issues faced by undocumented students make themselves available to answer specific questions and concerns such as "can they attend the university?" In the words of one Admission staff: "If a [undocumented] student approaches us, we certainly are very very willing to have that conversation, to let them know that it has nothing to do with whether or not you're going to get admitted to [university]" (JCU staff interview, 2011). Two interviewed staff spoke to this point, one of whom mentioned: "I will do my regular admissions presentation and then let them know that . . . if you have any questions about EOF [an equal opportunity program] or anything that requires the FAFSA, please feel free to come and speak to me afterwards, and usually when I give that heads up to the students they will stay behind" (JCU staff interview, 2011). Another interviewed staff mentioned that undocumented students "can be a little hesitant even about talking to an admissions counselor . . . because they don't know if this is going to have a negative impact on how their application is reviewed." In these cases, undocumented student hesitancy is countered by encouraging messaging: "Throw your hat into the ring, and see what happens" (JCU staff interview, 2011).

The messaging to students at JCUs is "Si Se Puede"/ "Yes We Can" (JCU staff interview, 2011). "Regardless of your immigration status or your status as a U.S. citizen, you are eligible—all students are eligible" (JCU staff interview, 2011). Interviewed staff indicated that their institutions welcome applications from all students regardless of their background. As one interviewed staff member mentioned: "Our university's current policy is that we will accept students from all over the world whatever their status is; they're free to apply (JCU staff interview, 2011).

ADMISSIONS & ENROLLMENT PROCESS

The admission policies of Jesuit institutions are inclusive. However only 30 of the 110 survey respondents indicated that there was some form of a process for enrolling undocumented students (Online survey of JCU staff, 2010–2011). Survey respondents indicated that all students go through the same application process. Practices are inclusive regardless of status: "We treat them as we would any other student" (JCU staff comment, online survey, 2010–2011). "The student is managed and handled like any other students" (JCU staff interview, 2011). Students are admitted "based on academic merit not immigration status" (JCU staff comment, online survey, 2010–2011).

Undocumented students apply to Jesuit institutions as any student would regardless of status. They engage in the standard admission process, a formal process that is the same for all students regardless of their immigration/citizenship status.

According to an interviewed staff member: "Generally the undocumented student is probably somebody who is presenting themselves to admissions just like any other student. So they've gone to a U.S. high school, they've taken the standardized tests—presenting all the same credentials as anybody else" (JCU staff interview, 2011). Students submit their application, high school credentials, test scores (sometimes optional), and recommendations from counselors and teachers.

Many schools use the common application or "Universal College Application," and one interviewer mentioned their institution uses their "own on-line application as well." One institution does not charge students to apply, and this policy appeals to undocumented students with limited financial resources (JCU staff interview, 2011).

JCU Staff on the Frontlines: Infrastructure of Support

Survey respondents identified their admissions, enrollment division, and international programs office as being responsible for communicating ad hoc policies internally. In terms of interactions, 58.1 percent of the surveyed staff have worked directly with undocumented students at their institution. When asked if specific admissions officers had direct responsibility to work with applications from undocumented students, 46 percent of admissions/enrollment staff answered "yes," and just over one-third (38 percent) said it was a "formal responsibility," versus 44 percent who indicated it was an informal policy (Online survey of JCU staff, 2010–2011).

When asked whom undocumented students turn to for assistance when they need help, staff listed a variety of offices with Campus Ministry (64 percent) and Diversity/Multicultural offices (53 percent) at the top, followed by Student Services and the Faculty (45 percent) (Online survey of JCU staff, 2010–2011). The most knowledgeable were admissions or enrollment staff, who have familiarity in working with undocumented students.

According to the staff interviews, university admissions' officers act as the "front door" for undocumented students to access Jesuit universities, working with each student "side by side" "in the trenches" (JCU staff interview, 2011) to figure out how to support a student from the time she or he is accepted, able to fund their college education, and enrolled as an undergraduate student. Admission staff are often part of on-campus and off-campus networks, interacting with colleagues across campus and the community beyond.

Three interviewed staff indicated that they worked closely with students during the application process. All mentioned there is a lot of communication with every applicant. In some cases, their work with undocumented students was particularly hands-on, as the students asked questions to verify that they were doing things correctly (e.g., should the student apply as a domestic or an international student?), and that their application is considered (JCU staff interview, 2011).

Two interviewed staff expressed concern over the limited information on points of contact available to undocumented students and the overall knowledge of infrastructures of support across campus.

> I tried to look on our website; we don't really have stuff on our website either to tell you where to go. I even thought, "Well gosh, where would I send a student?" And again, I just went back to, "Well, if it's around their social-personal adjustment, then I'll take care of it; but if it's around an academic issue then I'll give it to [other staff]." Other than the two of us, I couldn't think of where else I would go other than the two divisions of student development or academic affairs. (JCU staff interview, 2011)

This is problematic as undocumented students already approach the application process with many concerns, unsure of whom to turn to and whom they can trust. Eight interviewed staff commented on students being "fearful," "very nervous . . . scared" to open up to university staff, as "the student doesn't want to be outed" (JCU staff interview, 2011) or deported. Staff are attuned to the sensitivity of the issue. Two interviewed staff spoke of the delicate way in which referral contact is made with undocumented students in a "tactfully person-centered" way that allows students to disclose as much information as they feel comfortable doing (JCU staff interview, 2011).

Fear can be alleviated by an advocate and/or knowledgeable Admissions counselor who speaks openly with students and helps them through the application process. In addition, admissions officers often reach out to all students regardless of status to work with them individually to meet their admissions needs and make them feel comfortable:

> I try to keep as strong a connection as possible to students, especially those students who, not that I check to see if they have an alien

registration number put in, but I do try to make sure that all my students regardless of status know that I'm available to have any kind of conversation. I feel that when the student knows that they have that one person to speak to, you know, that they are assigned that one person in the admissions office, that gives them a comfort level to have a conversation, such as you know, their documentation. (JCU staff interview, 2011)

The intensity of working with undocumented students does not end with the application process; according to one interviewed staff, "You also have to be there to support them for months to make sure that they follow through and that they go to orientation and that they yield, which you do that with every student, but there is so much energy for that one student" (JCU staff interview, 2011).

Informal networks supporting undocumented students have emerged on campuses and into the community. Interviewed staff identified colleagues across campus who became part of a "very, very loose, very informal," "sort of ad hoc network" (JCU staff interview, 2011) that connects undocumented students or their advocates with the right campus contacts. At a small institution, one staff member indicated that many staff "just kind of pitch in" (JCU staff interview, 2011), and in one case an existing student group played an active role in reaching out to admitted undocumented students to welcome them into the community (JCU staff comment, online survey, 2010–2011).

The recognition and care for each individual student is reflected in one institution's motto of "one student at a time," which a staff member said was "painstakingly" put into practice (JCU staff interview, 2011). According to another staff, "Every student has their own story and theme, so we kind of work with each student and figure out, the best way for that student. We pick up the phone, we call one another . . ." (JCU staff interview, 2011).

The staff members active in informal campus networks and working most closely with undocumented students include those associated with student diversity programs, summer academic immersion programs, members of the Jesuit community, and admissions counselors.

Four interviewed staff commented on the importance of having an admissions point person who can work with undocumented students and maintain a network in the community. The admissions point person is someone "who knows what the policies and procedures are and how to approach negotiating the financial aid situation of that student." An interviewed staff spoke of a colleague who has become an informal point person, as having "a great rapport with students" and who "will maintain contact with them [undocumented students] and they will find their way into her office with some regularity" (JCU staff interview, 2011). Such point people need be knowledgeable of the infrastructure of support available on their campuses and aware of the particular barriers faced by undocumented students.

Institutional Challenges in Supporting Undocumented Students

JCUs face a number of challenges in supporting the needs of undocumented students. These include the ability of Jesuit institutions to provide financial and legal assistance to undocumented students, and ensuring staff awareness of institutional procedures vis-à-vis undocumented students and training staff to work with this specific population of students.

FINANCING HIGHER EDUCATION

Enrollment in a JCU is contingent on funding. With annual JCU tuition ranging from $28,060 to over $40,000 and the average cost of room and board between $10,000 and $20,000 (JCU staff comment, online survey, 2010–2011), it is not surprising that staff reported that cost and funding are the primary challenges faced in recruiting and enrolling undocumented students. The interviewed staff were aware of the great financial needs of undocumented students, "many require financial assistance as private institutions 'ain't cheap'" (JCU staff interview, 2011).

Surveyed staff indicated financial issues as the number one barrier of undocumented students to enrolling in a JCU with 77 respondents indicating affordability, tuition costs, and lack of financial aid and scholarships as challenges (Online survey of JCU staff, 2010–2011). Undocumented students experience "'sticker shock' at the cost of college and the challenge of paying for college when financial aid is not applicable and scholarships are limited" (JCU staff interview, 2011). Undocumented students may look into private institutions because they "didn't qualify for financial aid" elsewhere (JCU staff interview, 2011) and a Jesuit university can become "the school of last resort" (JCU staff interview, 2011).

Jesuit institutions do offer merit-based scholarships that do not stipulate a particular citizenship to be eligible, and universities can supplement with "ad hoc" funds. Money is pooled from a variety of private donor sources, including the Jesuit Community. At one JCU, up to twelve undocumented students received scholarships per year, though more often the number was lower, ranging from 2 to 5 students annually (JCU staff comment, online survey, 2010–2011), contingent on the availability of funds. A few institutions use development funds or special funding available through the president's office to support undocumented students.

Responsibility for authorizing aid to undocumented students is divided at many universities. Some leave the responsibility to the financial aid officers (48 percent) (JCU staff comment, online survey, 2010–2011). At other institutions the director of financial aid has responsibility (according to 60 percent of respondents). Admissions offices are involved at a number of universities and, at a few institutions, the president's office awards aid to undocumented students (JCU staff comment, online survey, 2010–2011). These stakeholders are critical as only slightly over 25 percent of survey respondents reported they were "fully-acquainted" with the financial aid process involving undocumented students (Online survey of JCU staff, 2010–2011).

At one institution, the Jesuit community has worked very closely with admissions on identifying outstanding undocumented students who have been accepted to the university and are potential scholarship candidates. As mentioned by one staff member in the Admissions' Office, "We have reached the point where we actually have a liaison in our own management who works with the Jesuit community to identify these students, and assist with making sure that the community is aware of the students' academic backgrounds and that person can work with the Financial Aid office as appropriate to see if there's any information we have about students" (JCU staff interview, 2011). However, the number of qualified applicants far outnumber the scholarships available, and most students do not receive a scholarship and subsequently do not attend the university. Admissions staff encourage students to seek out information, to do "their own research," talk to their high school counselor or talk to somebody about what financial options are available (JCU staff interview, 2011).

The reality is that financial demand is greater than what Jesuit institutions are able to provide. For instance, at one institution 140 undocumented students were contending for limited scholarship funds (JCU staff interview, 2011). Applications are scrutinized and ranked, and only "high achieving students," "the best of the best, the crème de la crème" are selected (JCU staff interview, 2011).

Financial aid options remain limited for undocumented students. They are not eligible for the "many federally funded programs that are there to help students get into college" (JCU staff interview, 2011). Financing their education is especially challenging for undocumented students as they generally cannot legally work for pay. Only 7 percent of staff reported that undocumented students can work on their campuses (Online survey of JCU staff, 2010–2011). Among the small number of respondents at institutions that provide work for undocumented students, they did not know which office or department is responsible for arranging work.

LEGAL INFRASTRUCTURE

The financial hurdle is not the only barrier in undocumented students "getting in the door" (JCU staff interview, 2011). Surveyed staff identified the lack of legal support services available at JCUs for undocumented students as problematic given the vulnerability and need of this student population. Without legal status, even physically accessing a campus location would be challenging without a driver's license. Similarly, in recruiting for career, the options of undocumented students would be limited to pursuing studies in which citizenship and fingerprinting are not required.

Three interviewed staff mentioned that navigating the issues of legal status and institutional practice can be tricky. Two staff recalled instances in which a student was in the process of being deported during the recruitment process and despite efforts to secure a visa, the university actors "were legally bound" to not allow the student to register (JCU staff interview, 2011).

Interviewed staff believed that their institutions should do more to provide legal assistance to undocumented students. About half of the survey respondents worked in a JCU that had a law school, and one-third (38 percent) reported that their institution had some connections with or sponsored a legal clinic providing assistance to the outside community (Online survey of JCU staff, 2010–2011). Only 10 percent reported that their university provided legal support for undocumented students to acquire citizenship (Online survey of JCU staff, 2010–2011). Sixty percent of the surveyed staff did not know or were unsure of whether their university provided legal assistance to undocumented students (Online survey of JCU staff, 2010–2011).

Dissemination of information regarding legal assistance, financial aid practices, and ad hoc policies to support undocumented students proved lacking. Information was limited to a few critical campus actors. This lack of staff awareness is noteworthy, and highlights the need for institutional infrastructures of communication and support to be put in place. Staff awareness of institutional procedures and campus resources is critical to meeting the diverse needs of undocumented students. Staff mentioned information sharing systems and training as important areas of development.

STAFF AWARENESS AND CAPACITY

As previously noted, few campus staff are well informed of institutional procedures and the needs of the undocumented student population. As one staff put it: "We don't have that infrastructure. I don't even think we have the institutional knowledge" (JCU staff interview, 2011). Those on the frontlines have learned "on the job" through their work with undocumented students (JCU staff interview, 2011).

To inform themselves of undocumented student needs, staff rely on dialogues with colleagues at regional and national professional conferences, some read articles, and share research and information through informal networks (JCU staff comments, online survey, 2010–2011). One interviewed staff mentioned informal conversations with admissions counselors informing them of undocumented student needs: "If there's something in the news about the DREAM Act or something like that, it'll come up and we'll discuss it; but nothing formal to say 'This is what the procedures are, this is the training'" (JCU staff interview, 2011).

Efforts are being made to inform campus actors on the needs of undocumented students. One staff member mentioned that their office "made a presentation to the faculty senate" (JCU staff interview, 2011) to inform faculty of issues surrounding undocumented students.

Little formal professional development was offered at most institutions. Only 11 percent of surveyed staff received or were aware of training. An additional 11 percent said that although training was available, they had not received it (Online survey of JCU staff, 2010–2011). Over three-quarters of respondents had not received training. Nor were they sure if training was available on their campus. Interviewed staff indicated the need for further knowledge on supporting undocumented students and institutional practices, as one stated: "I think I need to know more. If I want to help a student" (JCU staff interview, 2011).

Staff sensitive to undocumented student needs called for more formalized opportunities to build capacities in serving undocumented students, thus expanding networks of trust. As one staff mentioned, "I want to make sure that I'm not putting them in any kind of jeopardy" (JCU staff interview, 2011). Eleven staff spoke to the need for greater efforts on their campuses to formalize the dissemination of information on how best to work with undocumented students. Two interviewed staff called for training of staff on how best to work with the undocumented student population and meet their needs:

> I think it's a training issue . . . to work with any specific population I would think we'd need someone to come in and tell us, "What are some characteristics unique to this population." I can't even answer what specific legal issues there are. So, some background, some historical perspective, and then what is realistic, what are some things we can do to help this population. (JCU staff interview, 2011)

Assisting undocumented students requires being attuned to their needs and working across professional networks to find creative solutions for these students to access higher education. Overcoming institutional challenges in serving undocumented students and developing formal institutional policy for serving undocumented students would require an integrated effort across campus to share information so that all staff "are on the same page" (JCU staff interview, 2011).

A key finding of the research indicates that across all institutions, informal ad hoc systems are commonplace. Generally, a small number of university staff work closely with undocumented students. Regardless of their interaction with undocumented students, over 60 percent of the surveyed staff believed that educating undocumented students should be an institutional priority.

Jesuit Mission: Commitment to Serving Undocumented Students

Jesuit institutions are committed to inclusive excellence and diversity, as one interviewed staff indicated: "I think it's part of our mission to educate students, welcome students, provide home for all . . . so I think there's definitely a place in our mission statement to help these students" (Online survey of JCU staff, 2010–2011). As Jesuit institutions put their missions into practice, they take "non-discriminatory stands about students" (JCU staff comment, online survey, 2010–2011) and encourage students to apply regardless of their background.

Over 60 percent of staff strongly agreed or agreed that admitting, enrolling, and supporting undocumented students fit with the mission of Jesuit universities, and that it should be a focus of Jesuit higher education (see Chapter 4 for a more in-depth discussion of Jesuit mission).

Jesuit mission is reflected in the staff attitudes and efforts toward providing undocumented students with access to higher education. Interviewed staff recognized that undocumented students are often at a disadvantage when it comes to accessing higher education, as one staff mentioned: "These students are here and they have been and they could've been in the [city] district since Kindergarten. And they're working just as hard as someone that is documented; but they're not getting the advantages that someone documented would get, or they're not getting what we think as an individual they deserve" (JCU staff interview, 2011).

One interviewed staff member mentioned "a moral obligation to help these students" (JCU staff interview, 2011); another said, "I am totally committed to the idea of broad acts of higher education, and for me it's really allowing undocumented students who have gone to high school in the United States. [. . .] it's really a social justice issue. I mean the fact that their parents brought them here is not their fault" (JCU staff interview, 2011).

Many staff called upon their institution's Jesuit mission as influencing their beliefs and in guiding their informal practices in service of undocumented students. The opportunity to critically reflect on institutional practice helped some staff see that mission is not always put into practice, as one staff said: "We talk about *cura personalis*—care for the whole person, yet we're not doing it" (JCU staff interview, 2011). Commitment is conveyed through the actions taken by staff who work with undocumented students. Admissions staff were noted as the frontline of accessing higher education. Within these offices, an informally designated individual would put the institutional mission into practice and exude the Jesuit values as they work passionately with self-disclosed undocumented students, a process that requires a great deal of time and effort.

This openness to serving undocumented students appeared in staff comments when referring to their campuses as "more welcoming to undocumented immigrants" or a "sanctuary" for "high achieving undocumented students" (JCU staff interview, 2011).

Although staff values aligned with institutional mission, communicating clearly that a campus is welcoming of undocumented students is not something that is made explicit in official institutional practice, so as not to impact the perceptions of prospective students and families:

> As much as you want the university to be welcoming place for undocumented immigrants, it's a fine line, you know, university as a business. Because how does that look to for example, my daughter's junior in high school—we're looking around different schools for her to go to. For me, it wouldn't bother me, but I can see some of our neighbors, their kids, being suburban kids, looking at where they are going to . . . "Are we going to send the kids to school that has a reputation for being a haven for undocumented immigrants?" maybe not. (JCU staff interview, 2011)

In 2010, few institutions issued public messages of support for undocumented students; as a result, undocumented students may not have been aware that they could access JCUs. This lack of information was perhaps intentional as public perceptions and a conservative political atmosphere proved challenging given the controversial nature of immigration policy and reform. Institutions of higher education may have been concerned about making public their support of undocumented students, fearing the reprove of alumni, parents, donors, and enrolled students from privileged backgrounds. In this climate, undocumented students fear disclosing their status, may be apprehensive about joining campus communities that lack diversity, and are ill-equipped to provide a supportive and safe environment.

Staff work to realize the Jesuit educational mission to enroll and support undocumented students "to the full extent that the law allows" and in alignment with the institution's "religious and social justice mission" (JCU staff comment, online survey, 2010–2011). One interviewed staff felt that intentional recruitment of undocumented students would be true to the Jesuit mission given the limited opportunities to access higher education that this student population faces: "I think we are willfully under-utilizing our mission as a Jesuit institution that seeks justice, that seeks fairness. Diversity in our mission statement is prominently displayed as seeking God in all things. And here, in this particular way there is no God in the immigration system you know, that's fair to these students" (JCU staff interview, 2011). This same staff member knew of another "Catholic organization that has all the power in the world to do targeted recruitment of high-achieving undocumented students . . . and say, 'The doors are open for you here'" (JCU staff interview, 2011).

Many staff believed "in supporting students in receiving an integrated and transformative Jesuit education" and were "willing to be creative" in their approaches (JCU staff interviews, 2011). However, at the time this research was conducted, many staff thought their institutions proceeded cautiously, not making explicit statements to the public about their work with undocumented students, as a way to protect undocumented students in a political climate where immigration policies and issues proved controversial. Despite the norm of communicating under the radar, informal practices continue with active staff calling for more to be done through actions that align with institutional mission. This would require, as one interviewed staff mentioned, "to start appealing to our culture of equity, of fairness, of justice and our Catholic mission [. . .] to re-establish our Jesuit tradition and our Catholic nature" (JCU staff interview, 2011).

"Going Public": Making the Invisible Visible

When the research for the Ford-funded project[1] began in 2010, an Internet search of all twenty-eight Association of Jesuit Colleges and Universities (AJCU)[2] websites yielded little to no explicit mention of "undocumented" students. In informal discussions with staff at institutions, many mentioned that doing so could cause problems for the institution and might raise questions from some stakeholders including parents, prospective students, alumni, and donors. Staff also worried that having such information might put the few undocumented students already enrolled at risk. At the same time, staff recognized that Jesuit colleges have a tradition of educating the children of immigrants, a tradition that has historically helped many successful alumni of Jesuit institutions (JCU staff interview, 2011). JCU mission statements emphasize diversity, social responsibility, a focus on the whole student, creating men and women for others, and the promotion of social justice.

The collaborative research project between Fairfield University, Santa Clara University, and Loyola University Chicago on undocumented students in Jesuit universities throughout the U.S. and the dissemination of a summary report of the findings resulted in the raising of awareness across the JCUs and beyond. By going public on this pressing higher education issue, the twenty-eight schools in the Jesuit network acknowledged their efforts to be inclusive and welcoming to a marginalized population. The article "Should Colleges Help Undocumented Students? A Look at Why Many Catholic Institutions Are Doing Just That,"[3] featured in the *Chronicle of Higher Education* in 2014, referenced the research study and highlighted the role of faith-based institutions in supporting all students. Similarly, the website of the Society of Jesus posted an article entitled "Jesuit Colleges and Universities Help Undocumented Students Dream of a Better Future" (October 30, 2013).[4]

JCU INSTITUTIONAL COMMITMENT

Twenty-five presidents of Jesuit colleges released a statement in January 2013 indicating their institutions' commitment to supporting all students:

". . . we continue to affirm that Jesuit colleges and universities are morally committed environments, where our students are inspired and encouraged to understand and address issues of justice, fairness, political involvement, and a preferential option for those whom society has marginalized. We recognize that in 2013, one group that fits this category are those living without authorization in the United States. We will continue to support our students—both documented citizens and not—as full members of our campus communities and of society at large, where their voices and personal narratives deserve to be acknowledged."[5]

The presidents' public statement highlights how central the issue of serving all students is to their institutions' commitment to social justice and promoting equal access to higher education for all. By making a public statement, the JCU presidents are raising awareness to the issue of undocumented students in higher education. Their message informs multiple audiences including prospective undocumented students, campus faculty and staff, parents of enrolled students, and enrolled students. Leadership on the issue and stated commitment ensures that JCU staff can act accordingly, thereby validating their ad hoc practices in supporting undocumented students.

A CALL TO ACTION . . .

A few institutions took the research findings and the JCU presidents' statement as a call to action and have now made more public their efforts to make explicit the ways in which they welcome and support undocumented students. In Appendix A, we highlight institutional practices and efforts to support undocumented students. There is variety in what is considered public, but some institutions post their advocacy efforts, public statements of support, and information for prospective undocumented students. These institutional examples were informed by a web search conducted in April 2015.

The case study that follows provides a blueprint for what institutions can do to support undocumented students. It is based on the insights and collaborative work of Dr. Kaufka Walts, who is an active participant in several of the actions taken at Loyola University Chicago.

Loyola University Chicago (Illinois, Founded in 1870)—Case Study in Five Parts

Through strong leadership and collaboration between faculty, staff, and students, Loyola University Chicago has been striving to be a leader in working for educational opportunities for undocumented students, including those who identify with the DREAMer community, DACA-status, and DACA-eligible students. The University's efforts include our current chancellor and former president, Michael Garanzini, S.J.'s, public statements supporting undocumented student access to higher education; the pathbreaking work of the Stritch School of Medicine as the first medical school in the nation to openly accept qualified undocumented students; the development of "Share the DREAM" safe space and ally training through the Department of Student Diversity and Multicultural Affairs (SDMA); and the launch by SDMA in fall 2013 of an "Undocumented Student Resource" webpage; a task force, University Collaborative for Undocumented Students ("UCUS") to review and reflect on the research report, "Immigration: Undocumented Students in Higher Education," authored by Santa Clara University, Fairfield University, and Loyola University Chicago, and a subsequent appointment of a standing committee to implement the recommendations of the UCUS report and to support ongoing efforts on behalf of undocumented students (including DACA [Deferred Action for Childhood Arrivals] and DACA-eligible individuals) at Loyola University Chicago and beyond.

To provide readers with an example of how an institution can address the issues raised by students and staff in increasing the success and experience of students who are undocumented in higher education, we present an in-depth case study. This five-part case study provides an overview of Loyola University Chicago's current efforts to support undocumented, DACA and DACA-eligible students, and provides examples across all departments, schools, and divisions within higher education institutions.

Part 1: "Share the Dream" Ally Training (2012—Present), University-Wide Education and Ally Building

On June 15, 2012, the Obama administration announced the Deferred Act for Childhood Arrivals (DACA) program for eligible DREAMers to apply for Deferred Action. Deferred Action would provide protection from removal, access to work authorization (and a Social Security number), and in some states, a driver's license and state identification card. In light of this announcement, the Department of Student Diversity and Multicultural Affairs (SDMA) created a training for Loyola University Chicago faculty and students with the goal to teach more about the history, struggles, and needs of undocumented students, and to bring awareness, build safe spaces, and provide allies with resources to support undocumented, DREAMer, and DACA students within Loyola University Chicago.

Content includes an overview of the DREAMer movement, national statistics and research, and introduction to DACA and other legal terminology related to undocumented students. It also includes criteria for eligibility, Loyola University Chicago formal support of undocumented students via public statements made by President Michael Garanzini, S.J., an introduction to the diversity of experiences of undocumented students, case studies, discussion of privilege and identity to frame appropriate interventions, and support for undocumented students, campus partners, and campus and national resources. Individuals who participate in the training are eligible for an Ally card (participants must sign an Ally agreement that confirms their understanding of this role) to display in their office to show a visible safe space for members of this population at Loyola. To date, 367 participants have been trained on campus.

In conjunction with the Safe Ally trainings, the Department of Student Diversity and Multicultural Affairs also launched the Undocumented Student Resource web page. This web page was developed in an effort to provide a centralized and public location for undocumented students and their families to find information about Loyola University Chicago support of the DREAMer movement, education for undocumented students, and links to both the Office of Admissions and the Office of Financial Aid, as well as national resources.

Part 2: Loyola University Stritch School of Medicine—First School in the Country to Accept Qualified Undocumented Students (2013)

Adapted from school website "DREAMers of DACA Status Welcome"[6]

A diverse medical workforce is very important to the health of our communities for reasons that are well known. Physicians who share ethnic, cultural, or racial backgrounds with underserved patients are more likely to choose to serve those underserved populations, produce improved outcomes, and can become role models within the community. In addition, it is desirable that all physicians develop a level of cultural sensitivity and competence. Training side-by-side in a diverse student body can foster understanding of persons and cultures different from one's own. Thus, increasing diversity benefits all students.

The Stritch School of Medicine at Loyola University Chicago recognized undocumented students as an untapped resource for both the medical profession and medical education. However, lack of work authorization and status prohibited licensure to practice medicine, presenting a huge obstacle to accessing medical education and practice. Prior to the creation of the Deferred Action for Childhood Arrivals (DACA) program in 2012, any DREAMer who graduated medical school would be unable to secure a work authorization and a social security number. Thus, he or she would be unable to gain a license to practice medicine and enter residency training. Medical schools understandably had been reluctant to accept and educate students who would not be able to treat patients. Such a situation would consume significant resources of the educational institution without meeting its goal, namely, to produce physicians to serve the community's patient populations.

With the Presidential Executive Order creating Deferred Action for Childhood Arrivals (DACA) in 2012, the Stritch School of Medicine saw DACA status as removing a long-standing barrier to securing a residency slot—medical school graduates who have DACA status will be eligible to gain a state license[7] to practice medicine and thereby enter a residency training program. The Stritch School of Medicine, Loyola University Chicago, identified DREAMer students with DACA-status as a potential source of qualified and diverse talent that will be an asset to the medical education environment, the medical profession, and patients. These young people are often bicultural and bilingual and possess insight into the immigrant experience. In a nation that has a large immigrant population, these young people can help to foster the ability of the physician workforce to treat the array of patients they will encounter in their practices. The School of Medicine amended its admissions policies to include qualified students who have received DACA status.

The immediate obstacle that DREAMers faced *after* acceptance to the Stritch Medical School (and all medical schools), however, is financing their medical education. Students with DACA status remain ineligible for most federal benefits including federal loans. Such loans comprise an important part of a typical medical student's financial aid package. To help address this challenge, the Illinois Finance Authority (IFA) created a DACA loan program modeled after public health service loans. This is available to the state's seven medical and three dental schools and requires students who access the program to provide a year of service in a designated underserved area of Illinois for each year of the loan. This loan requires that the recipient provide a year of service in a designated underserved area of the State of Illinois for each year he or she receives the loan. The loan is interest-free with completion of the service obligation. This loan program is designed to enhance the physician infrastructure of the state and provide much-needed services to Illinois residents in serious need. Because the IFA does not rely on taxpayer funding, no tax dollars support this loan program.

In August 2014, the Stritch School of Medicine welcomed its first cohort of seven DREAMer medical students to the class of 2016, making history as the first medical school in the country to admit "DREAMer" students. All of the DREAMer students competed on a level playing field throughout the admissions process with every other applicant to the medical school, and were admitted on their academic achievements and merits. "Our social justice tradition called us to take a leadership role in offering educational opportunities to underserved groups, including qualified applicants with DACA status. We also believe that the mission to train a talented and diverse physician workforce should motivate other medical schools to do the same. The opportunities are now much greater than the barriers," said Linda Brubaker, MD, MS, dean, and chief diversity officer.

Part 3: University Task Force—"University Collaborative for Undocumented Students" (UCUS)

In the beginning of the 2013–2014 academic year, the President's Cabinet asked that a University-wide committee be created to assess the University's current work regarding undocumented, Deferred Action for Childhood Arrivals (DACA), and DACA-eligible students, and explore ideas from the research presented in part one of this chapter and Chapter 5, enhance collaboration, serve as a "point of contact" for those inside as well as those outside the University, and provide recommendations for the University moving forward. The group, to be called "University Collaborative for Undocumented Students" ("UCUS") was chaired by Kathleen Maas Weigert (Professor of Women and Leadership and Assistant to the Provost for Social Justice Initiatives). She appointed a Steering Committee (SC): Phil Hale (Government Affairs), Katherine Kaufka Walts (Center for the Human Rights of Children), Mark Kuczewski (Stritch School of Medicine), and Sadika Sulaiman Hara (Student Diversity and Multicultural Affairs).

The UCUS committee was comprised of fifteen faculty, staff, and student representatives (including an undocumented graduate student) across all three campuses, representing seven university departments and schools, and a final group was created. A shared site was also created for UCUS members to share resources, materials, and ideas. Four subcommittees were created to reflect areas of focus emerging from our discussions: 1) Institutional Practices and Policies, 2) Website, 3) Resources for Students and Faculty, and 4) Outreach. The UCUS met five times, examined current activities, explored lacunae, and proposed recommendations.

Before a more detailed discussion of the work and outcomes of the UCUS committee, it is important to share that the discussion and efforts by the UCUS Committee were grounded in the framework provided by the Catholic and Jesuit mission to promote social justice with the bedrock principle being one of acceptance of undocumented students as part of Loyola's broader culture of acceptance, inclusion, safety and support. Similar to the process by which the Stritch School of Medicine's actions were founded in Catholic and Jesuit principles of social justice, at each UCUS meeting, discussion of the broader university and values took place as a framework for activities by the Committee. A values statement was drafted to include in the final report[8]:

> The recommendations contained in this report are grounded in the Catholic and Jesuit mission to promote social justice and in the bedrock principle, that acceptance of undocumented students is part of Loyola University Chicago's broader culture of acceptance, inclusion, safety and support. As a Catholic university that is sponsored by the Society of Jesus (the Jesuits), we firmly believe in the dignity of each person and in the promotion of social justice. The dignity of persons calls us to steward the talents of qualified applicants rather than reject their contributions for arbitrary and arcane reasons, including immigration status. Social justice requires that we foster the conditions for full participation in the community by all members of our community. Undocumented, DACA, and DACA-eligible applicants are typically woven into the fabric of our communities and have a basic right to contribute to the fullest extent of their abilities. This approach echoes a long tradition articulated by the U.S. Conference of Catholic Bishops (USCCB) of advocacy for immigrant members of our communities. (UCUS University Task Force Report, 2014)

The outcomes of the UCUS committee work were twofold: 1) a brief snapshot of current Loyola activities around the university addressing issues pertaining to undocumented and DREAMer students, and 2) recommendations for the university moving forward. For the purpose of this chapter, the twenty recommendations have been adapted from the original UCUS report, and as applicable, a brief discussion follows each recommendation with an update regarding its status.

The twenty recommendations are organized around several interrelated themes and issues representing areas in which the University can utilize its resources to promote educational opportunity and inclusion for undocumented undergraduate and graduate students and graduates. The organizational framework of the recommendations follows the process of admission to, matriculation in, and graduation from the university. The recommendations include efforts to improve communication and resources, promote academic endeavors, and develop appropriate policies and further research.

The recommendations were promulgated in recognition of the dedicated and multifaceted efforts it would take—University-wide—to implement the remaining recommendations. A dedicated, multidisciplinary standing committee, comprised of administrators, faculty, and students representing all facets of student life, was required to advance the University's mission, to develop the institutional policies and practices described below, as well as advise the Provost Office on issues related to undocumented students as they arose.

At the time of publication, several of the recommendations have been implemented (see Appendix B for a list of twenty recommendations). For example, in April, 2015, then Provost, John Pelissero, appointed Katherine Kaufka Walts (Director, Center for the Human Rights of Children) and Mark Kuczewski (Stritch School of Medicine) to Co-Chair this standing Committee (See "Part 5: "Promoting Dignity Through Education"). To date, Loyola University Chicago has committed to providing five, full-ride scholarships to undergraduate students, and hope to increase the number of scholarships in subsequent years. Additionally, the inaugural class of Arrupe College, Loyola University Chicago's two-year college granting associate degrees, is providing thirty-five undocumented students with full funding.

Part 4: Student Leadership & Commitment to Access
to Higher Education for Undocumented Students:
The Magis Scholarship Fund (2015)

In addition to formal measures by university administrators and faculty noted above, Loyola University Chicago students have demonstrated their commitment to access to higher education for their undocumented, DACA, and DACA-eligible peers through the formation of a new financial aid opportunity/scholarship. Recognizing that one of the largest obstacles in access to higher education for undocumented students is financial resources, in the summer of 2014, the Student Government of Loyola Chicago (SGLC) partnered with the Latin American Student Organization (LASA) to create a scholarship fund for undocumented Loyola undergraduate students. SGLC and LASA created a campaign to support the initiative and raise broader awareness amongst the undergraduate student population. Approximately 70 percent of student voters subsequently approved a referendum[9] that would increase their semester fees by $2.50 per semester to allocate to a scholarship fund for undocumented students who cannot receive state or federal financial aid and demonstrate financial need. After several meetings with Loyola's Donor Relations Office and Office of Financial Aid, the Magis Scholarship fund officially launched in 2015.

Former student body president Flavio Bravo, one of the champions of the Magis Scholarship fund, stated, "It says, 'Here at Loyola we accept the best and the brightest no matter what their documentation is.'" Bravo was also a member of the "UCUS Committee" referred above, which spurred his interest in mobilizing students around this issue to develop concrete ways to advance educational opportunities for undocumented students.

The increased fees—$5 per student per year, for a total of more than $50,000—would support the Magis Scholars Fund, named after the Latin word for "more." The student government and Latin American Student Organization will oversee and award the money. Applicants would need to be full-time undergraduates with a GPA of 3.0 or higher, and demonstrate financial need and leadership potential.

This extraordinary effort undertaken by the undergraduate student population is inspiring similar student movements at other campuses. Additionally, conversations have started about how faculty can support the student initiative with designated donations to the Magis Scholarship Fund, as well as other fundraising opportunities on campus.

Part 5: DREAMer Committee: Promoting Dignity Through Education, the Appointment of a Standing University Committee (2015)

In April 2015, the Provost formally appointed members of a University Standing Committee, the "DREAMer Committee" to oversee the implementation of the UCUS report recommendations. The mission of the DREAMer Committee is to develop equitable policies and practices to promote educational opportunities and success of undocumented students at Loyola University Chicago. This will be achieved through multidisciplinary collaboration and the promotion of research, education, advocacy, and service that is informed by the lives and experiences of undocumented students seeking higher education.

The DREAMer Committee is a university-wide standing committee that succeeds the task force (UCUS Committee) (see "Part 2") that reviewed Loyola's progress in meeting the needs of these students. The task force found that Loyola University Chicago had become an emerging national leader in promoting equity for these students. Achievements included the Stritch School of Medicine becoming the first U.S. medical school to openly welcome DREAMers (www.stritch.luc.edu/daca) and the incredible undergraduate effort that create the Magis Scholarship Fund for DREAMers from a self-imposed student activity fee. Such "firsts" have brought the university renown and highlighted the value all levels of the university place on social justice. However, progress was uneven across the schools of the university, and dedicated attention needed to be given to these issues. The collaboration of dedicated faculty, administrators, and students is needed to further opportunity for DREAMers at Loyola and to seek systemic change in our nation's immigration system through scholarship and advocacy.

The committee is currently comprised of eighteen faculty, staff, and student representatives (including undocumented students) from all campuses, professional schools, and colleges represented. The Committee Co-Chairs and University leadership believed it is important to include the student voice and perspective as part of the committee's work. As noted above, at time of publication, several of the UCUS Report recommendations have been implemented under this DREAMer committee. We hope the work of the committee addresses critical issues raised in the findings from the JCU research study addressed in Part 2 of this chapter, as well as Loyola University Chicago's own examinations on this issue via the UCUS task force to promote access, including improved communication, support, and educational outcomes for undocumented, DACA, and DACA-eligible students.

Conclusion

Our intention in presenting the perspective of staff at Jesuit universities in the U.S. as well as an in-depth case study is to provide concrete and measureable strategies, tactics, and examples that can potentially be used by other institutions.

Based on the research findings, Jesuit college policies and practices in recruiting, enrolling, and supporting undocumented students were for the most part invisible, "off the radar," ad hoc, and involved a small network of committed people. In 2010, few institutions were public about their work with undocumented students, and few institutional websites featured information on the topic or used the term "undocumented." As a result of this research and dissemination of findings, greater awareness has been raised both on and off campuses regarding the role and commitment of JCUs in helping undocumented students fulfill their dreams of a college degree. Higher education offers few options for undocumented students and JCUs provide one entry point for a marginalized population. Surveyed and interviewed staff were able to reflect on their institution's policies, staff capacities, and what they could be doing better to meet the needs of undocumented students, taking action to promote social justice, inclusiveness, and access for all.

Despite the challenges faced by undocumented students and the informal nature of higher education practices, Jesuit schools are making strides to help undocumented students overcome barriers and access higher education. The case study is an example of putting social justice in action via institutional practices as related to our common mission—educating the "whole person" and fostering inclusive communities of excellence. The Loyola University Chicago case provides a blueprint for institutions looking for ways to support undocumented students. The

elements of the plan—assessing institutional capacity to support undocumented students, establishing infrastructure of support, communicating
explicitly the policies regarding admission of undocumented students, for-
malizing institutional contacts, including student voice in policies developed, providing web resources to communicate to prospective and current
students, exploring financial aid options, training staff and students, and
engaging in and influencing statewide and national dialogue to reflect Jesuit values—are approaches that can be adapted to any campus striving
to be more accessible to a diverse student body.

In all of the initiatives mentioned, Loyola's process included reflection
and iteration of institutional values, and keen attention paid to what undocumented students told us—via research and their lived experience—
about their process accessing higher education. We hope other universities
can glean ideas and apply versions of the above at their own campus. It is
important to note that while the activities described above occurred at
Loyola University Chicago, they are part of a broader context of activities,
research, reflection, and advocacy work on behalf of all Jesuit colleges and
universities, including the research outlined earlier.

We are constantly learning from research, our partners, our students,
and other institutions about promising practices, opportunities to improve,
and other ways to improve educational outcomes for all members of our
community, in this case, undocumented students. It is clear that administrators, faculty, and students are passionate about this issue, and we are
all on the forefront of a larger movement to accompany undocumented
students to a more accepting, inclusive, and supportive path to higher
education.

Appendix A

Example of JCUs' Public Support of Undocumented Students

University of San Francisco (California, founded in 1855)

The University of San Francisco (USF) hosts a web page of resources to
support current prospective undocumented students through their Division of Student Life. The opening statement on the page is "Uncompro-

mising, undeterred, unbiased—the University of San Francisco is committed to helping undocumented students bolster their future as citizens of the world. We're speaking out for students who are inspired to change the world from here."[10] The site highlights the institution's commitment, its network of USF Allies[11]—faculty and administrators dedicated to helping undocumented students navigate the university, information, and FAQs on the application and financial aid process, information on legislation (rights, DREAM Act, Deferred Action for Childhood Arrivals, and other legislation), and other resources, news, research, and terminology. This website was the result of a USF Task Force on Support and Services for Undocumented Students created by the Diversity Office in January 2014. The Task Force provided recommendations and an overview of resources available for undocumented students at USF.

Seattle University (Washington, founded in 1891)

At Seattle University, the Office of Multicultural Affairs (OMA) hosts an "Undocumented Student Resources" page. As stated at the top of the page "The Office of Multicultural Affairs at Seattle University works with all members of the university community in a social justice framework to promote the leadership formation, wellness, and success of students of color and queer students, regardless of their status in this country. Recognizing that undocumented students make important contributions to the intellectual and social life of the campus, Seattle University admits and enrolls students regardless of citizenship."[12] The OMA compiled resources from nonprofit local and national organizations, services, and other educational information to support undocumented students. The site also includes subpages on scholarships for undocumented students to help pay for tuition; the Scarlett U Campaign launched in 2012 "with the intent to create a safe space for students who are undocumented, and to share with those who have a strong commitment to create a community of care, and confidentiality, for all students regardless of their status in this country."[13] Additionally a subpage that highlighted the NASPA Region V Drive-in Conference hosted at Seattle University on October 22, 2012, bringing together student affairs professionals from higher education institutions to "address the ways in which student affairs professionals from all higher education institutional types can understand and support undocumented students."[14] These resources and institutional activities include advocacy, making resources and information explicit, and a "train the trainers" model of professional development for University staff.

Marquette University (Wisconsin, founded in 1881)

Marquette University's Career Services Center offers a list of resources for undocumented students on its website.[15] Resources include: career resources, DACA resources, local legal resources, and a "submit a question" field. Marquette also has a page providing resources for high school guidance counselors.[16] This includes a statement "undocumented students are eligible to apply for admission into Marquette and for scholarship consideration." The site features a PDF document "Marquette guide to the application and scholarship process for undocumented students"[17] and a link to the College Board's "Advising Undocumented Students" on admissions and financial aid.

Regis University (Colorado, founded in 1877)

The President of Regis University issued a public policy statement "Letter to the Regis University Community Regarding Immigration Reform and Support for Undocumented Students" (March 15, 2013)[18] supporting inclusive public policy, immigration issues, and encouraging the Regis community to engage on the topic of undocumented students in higher education. Additionally, to address the financial challenges of accessing higher education, the Regis University Financial Aid office provides information on applying for aid and explicitly states its support of undocumented students: "Regis University is dedicated to providing financial support to undocumented students within the limits of state and federal law. (. . .) Regis University provides institutional funds to undocumented students by awarding academic and other talent-based scholarships."[19]

Loyola Marymount (California, founded in 1911)

Financing a college degree proves challenging for undocumented students. At Loyola Marymount, the Office of Ethnic & Intercultural Services in the Student Affairs Division provides a resource website[20] including links to organizations offering scholarships and informational resources for undoc-umented students such as organizations, centers, and institutes advocat-ing for undocumented students (referred to as AB 540 students in the state of California), toolkits, and guides to assist undocumented students and their families with college financial planning.

Georgetown University (Washington, D.C., founded in 1789)

At Georgetown University, the Office of Undergraduate Admissions pro-vides information for International Applicants and includes a section for undocumented students stating, "The application process for Undocu-mented students is exactly the same as for any other candidate, regard-less of country of citizenship or where the student resides or attends high school. Georgetown's need-blind admissions process and holistic review applies to all applicants: U.S. Citizens, U.S. Permanent Residents, Foreign Citizens and Undocumented students. The holistic admissions process means that a variety of factors beyond a student's grades and standard-ized testing are carefully considered by the Committee on Admissions. Undocumented students should feel comfortable providing as much in-formation as possible on the application forms. Their status is not a 'neg-ative' factor in the admissions process. In the event you, your parents or college counselor have any questions about the admissions process, dead-lines or requirements, we encourage you to contact our office."[21]

Saint Peter's University (New Jersey, founded in 1872)

In November 2014, Saint Peter's University announced the opening of its Center for Undocumented Students.[22] The mission of The Center for Undocumented Students (TCUS) is to provide academic support to un-documented students enrolled at Saint Peter's University, bring attention to political and policy issues around immigration, and create a community that welcomes undocumented students. The TCUS creates a network on and off campus in order to improve access and retention of undocumented students in higher education. Additionally, TCUS developed curriculum and programming to support faculty, administrators, and staff in their pro-fessional development. The TCUS emerged from a coalition at Saint Peter's comprised of the Public Policy Program, the Social Justice Program, and the Guarini Institute for Government and Leadership, the Department of Sociology and Urban Studies, the Department of Political Science, the Department of Education, Campus Ministry, the Africana Studies Program, the Women's Studies Program, and the Latin American/Latino Studies Program.

Fairfield University (Connecticut, founded in 1942)

In 2010, Fairfield University embarked on a research study "Immigration: Undocumented Students in Higher Education" in collaboration with Santa Clara University and Loyola University Chicago. Fairfield's Center for Faith & Public Life at Fairfield University hosts a website that provides access to the research findings and recommendations, FAQs, emerging practices, resources (local, legal, fellowship/internships, college support, and advocacy).[23]

Santa Clara University (California, founded in 1851)

At the time of the collaboration on the 2010–2012 research study, it was public knowledge that the Hurtado Scholars Program, a scholarship program supported by the Jesuit Community at Santa Clara, provided access for undocumented students. However, at the time of the writing of this chapter the link to the program was offline, and no information about the scholarship was available on the Santa Clara website. The Santa Clara University Career Center continues to host a website of resources for undocumented students.[24]

Appendix B

University Collaborative for Undocumented Students (UCUS) Recommendations (20)

Adapted from the UCUS Report[25] presented to the Provost, Council of Deans, and Cabinet, Health Sciences Division Cabinet, November 2014.

1. Create a University-wide Standing Committee charged with advancement of the goals articulated in this report and the implementation of any recommendations that flow from it. As part of its

responsibility, the Committee should continue to seek equality of opportunity without regard to immigration status in all of Loyola's initiatives.

A. Additional recommendations—categorized by issue:

ISSUE: The largest hurdle for undocumented students to obtain higher education is access to financial resources. Undocumented students are not eligible for federal financial aid.

RECOMMENDATIONS:

2. Determine a specific number of undocumented students that the University can fully fund via internal resources and communicate this information to the University community and to our external constituencies.

3. Ensure that the necessary expertise exists in Admissions and Financial Aid and Student Services Hub offices to help undocumented, DACA, and DACA-eligible students navigate the various systems and access all available aid. Counsel such students on financial aid eligibility and take steps to maximize financial aid opportunities for them.

ISSUE: In addition to financial aid, undocumented students often face uncertainties navigating the Loyola University Chicago admission process, including eligibility to apply and the online application system.

RECOMMENDATIONS:

4. As part of the recruitment and enrollment process, communicate clearly Loyola's commitment to admitting undocumented students. Ensure that admissions personnel include undocumented students in their standard outreach and recruitment presentations.

    *"Loyola welcomes applications from all potential students,
    including but not limited to, their race, ethnicity, religion,
    gender, disability, sexual orientation, or immigration status."*

5. Change the current online admissions process to facilitate applications from undocumented students without regard to immigration status, including information about restrictions for federal financial aid.

Example: In the application management system, Slate, include
"Please select the Visa you will be on to attend Loyola. If you
are an undocumented student, a student eligible for deferred
action or are uncertain, please select 'other.'"

At the time of publication, these recommendations have been implemented. The "DREAMer Standing Committee" is currently exploring ways to conduct broader outreach about our undergraduate scholarships to the broader community, including high school counselors, families, and communities across the country.

ISSUE: Admitted undocumented students face many challenges on campus, including continued financial support, social and emotional assistance, safety, and help integrating into academic, co-curricular, professional activities, and other opportunities. These students need ongoing resources and support to participate fully in student life and to promote their right to safety, privacy, and educational opportunities.

RECOMMENDATIONS:

6. Following the example of the Stritch School of Medicine, each College and School should explore the possibility of adopting the Medical School approach, which would include not only accepting DACA and DACA-eligible students, but also providing financial support and opportunities for professional licensing (including, but not limited to, nursing, law, social work, education, and psychology) to qualified persons with DACA immigration status or who are DACA-eligible.

   Example: Undocumented, DACA and DACA-eligible students are
   precluded from admission to practice law under most state bars
   (California being the current exception), in contrast to the
   path to practice medicine as identified by Loyola's Stritch
   School of Medicine.

7. Identify a point of contact in each College and School to be informed of current federal and state laws regarding professional practice for this group of students, and to receive appropriate training regarding the rights and needs of undocumented students, including academic, professional, and co-curricular activities.

*Example: Undocumented students are barred from federal
employment (including research fellowships) and internships,
but may be able to pursue both paid and unpaid employment
at local and state public offices.*

8. Explore an "exit interview" or similar opportunity to both learn about undocumented students' experiences at Loyola, and to provide career counseling about what professional and/or academic opportunities students are (and are not) eligible for upon graduation.

9. Building on the resources developed by Student Diversity and Multicultural Affairs,[26] develop a comprehensive website addressing related topics, including definitions, federal and state laws, tuition, admissions and financial aid, student housing, student health insurance and support, academic and other specialized advising and counseling services, student leadership, experiential work opportunities, and other local and national resources, FAQs, and Loyola contact information. This website should be readily available to prospective (including links to admissions) as well as current undocumented students, and updated annually.

10. Develop and offer "Know Your Rights" workshops and materials addressing resources, safety and well-being, and experiential learning and career opportunities (internships, externships, part-time, or summer employment), that undocumented students can and cannot apply for. These informational workshops should also be available to faculty, staff, and students to broaden institutional knowledge and support networks for undocumented students.

11. Explore the possibility of creating a "sanctuary" campus for all first responders. Meaning, create a policy prohibiting all campus safety, medical, and wellness center staff from inquiring as to a student's immigration status.

*Example: Ensure all students know that the student health plan
is open to undocumented and DACA students, and that all
university services require only a student ID, not a social
security number.*

12. Ensure the Office for International Programs (and the counterpart at Medical School) and faculty leading international alternative service/immersion and study abroad trips include explicit policies alerting undocumented students to risks of traveling internationally, including potential bars to re-admission to the United States.

ISSUE: Hiring policies and alumni networking are important areas to make the University's work comprehensive.

RECOMMENDATIONS:

13. Clarify Loyola's Human Resources policies regarding hiring employees with DACA status, including faculty and staff.

14. Encourage every College and School's alumni unit to create a process for undocumented, or formerly undocumented, alums to mentor incoming students.

ISSUE: The challenges facing undocumented students and families in our communities require ongoing academic research to increase knowledge and improve practices related to undocumented students.

RECOMMENDATIONS:

15. Encourage and support faculty research, teaching, outreach, and service learning initiatives aimed at exploring or illuminating issues of relevance to migration, immigration, and the lived experience of undocumented students. Assist faculty to secure external funding to support such endeavors.

16. Publish an annual report on the status of undocumented students at Loyola to support ongoing advocacy efforts (including Student Affairs and Enrollment Management among others) across both Maywood and Lakeside campuses. This process should include a review of policies, procedures, and resources to ensure they are current and accurate.

ISSUE: The importance of collaboration among the JCU schools is imperative to advance the cause of undocumented students.

RECOMMENDATIONS:

17. As proposed in the Fairfield/Loyola/Santa Clara report, the University should look into the idea of "a 'Common Fund' to raise money to support undocumented students at all Jesuit institutions" (p. 16).

18. To broaden our understanding of the issues, we recommend initiating a "Phase 2" of the Fairfield/Loyola/Santa Clara study, and survey Illinois institutions of higher education to identify current policies and practices related to DREAMer students.

ISSUE: The importance of working for policies to advance immigration reform is critical to advance meaningful, long-term solutions to challenges facing undocumented students and their families.

RECOMMENDATIONS:

19. Publicize the fact that President Garanzini, S.J., along with over one hundred other Catholic College presidents, has signed onto a letter supporting immigration reform with a path to citizenship.

20. The University continues to contribute to local and national policy efforts that support undocumented students.

Notes

1. Fairfield University, Loyola University Chicago, Santa Clara University. (2013). Immigrant Student National Position Paper: Report on Findings, January 2013. Retrieved from http://www.fairfield.edu/academics /schoolscollegescenters/academiccenters/centerforfaithandpubliclife /generatingresearch-basedsolutions/immigrantstudentproject/.

2. Association of Jesuit Colleges and Universities (2015). Member institutions and Jesuit College and University map. Retrieved from http://www .JCUnet.edu/institutions#map.

3. D. M. Perry (2014). "Should Colleges Help Undocumented Students? A Look at Why Many Catholic Institutions Are Doing Just That," July 21, 2014. *The Chronicle of Higher Education.* Retrieved from http://chronicle.com/article/ Should-Colleges-Help/147809/.

4. Society of Jesus (2013). Jesuit Colleges and Universities Help Undocumented Students Dream of a Better Future, October 30, 2013. Featured on the Jesuit Conference website. Retrieved from http://jesuits.org/story?tn=project -20131023114628.

5. University of San Francisco, Division of Student Life. JCU presidents' statement, January 2013. Retrieved from https://www.usfca.edu/studentlife /undocumented/JCU-presidents-statement/.

6. DREAMers of DACA Status Welcome, Stritch School of Medecine, Loyola University Chicago Health Sciences Division. Retrieved from http:// ssom.luc.edu/daca/.

7. N. N. Sawicki (2013). "Doctors Who DREAM: Clearing up Confusion on Citizenship Requirements," Bill of Health, a blog by the Petrie-Flom Center examining the intersection of law and health care, biotech, and bioethics, Harvard Law. Posted on September 24, 2013. Retrieved from http://blogs.law .harvard.edu/billofhealth/2013/09/24/doctors-who-dream-clearing-up -confusion-on-citizenship-requirements/.

8. UCUS Report available online. "Promoting Human Rights of Undocumented Students," Center for the Human Rights of Children, Loyola University Chicago. Retrieved from http://www.luc.edu/chrc/childrenandyouthnavigating systemsalone/promotinghumanrightsofundocumentedstudents/.

9. Student Government of Loyola University Chicago (Spring 2015). Magis Scholarship Referenda Resolution. Retrieved from http://issuu.com /sgloyolachicago/docs/magis_scholarship_legislation__1_.

10. University of San Francisco, Division of Student Life. Undocumented Student Resources. Retrieved from https://www.usfca.edu/studentlife /undocumented.

11. University of San Francisco, Division of Student Life. Undocumented Student Allies. Retrieved from https://www.usfca.edu/studentlife /undocumented/usf-allies/.

12. Seattle University, Office of Multicultural Affairs. Undocumented Student Resources. Retrieved from https://www.seattleu.edu/oma/resources /undocumented/.

13. Seattle University, Office of Multicultural Affairs. Scarlett U Campaign. Retrieved from https://www.seattleu.edu/oma/success/undocumented /campaign/.

14. Seattle University, Office of Multicultural Affairs. NASPA Region V Drive In Conference. Retrieved from https://www.seattleu.edu/oma/success /undocumented/naspa/.

15. Marquette University, Career Services Center. Resources for Undocumented Student. Retrieved from http://www.marquette.edu/csc/resources /undocumentedstudents.shtml.

16. Marquette University, Career Services Center. Resources for Guidance Counselors. Retrieved from http://www.marquette.edu/explore/school -counselor.php.

17. Marquette University, Career Services Center. Application and Scholarship Guide for Undocumented Students. Retrieved from http://www.marquette.edu/explore/documents/undocumented-students.pdf.

18. Regis University (2013). Public Policy statement from the Office of the President at Regis University. "Letter to the Regis University Community Regarding Immigration Reform and Support for Undocumented Students," March 15, 2013. Retrieved from http://www.regis.edu/About-Regis-University/Regis-University-Leadership/Office-of-the-President/Communications/Public-Policy.aspx.

19. Regis University (2015). Office of Financial Aid. Undocumented Student Financial Support. Retrieved from http://www.regis.edu/College-Admissions-and-Financial-Aid/College-Financial-Aid/Applying-for-Aid.aspx.

20. Loyola Marymount, Office of Ethnic and Intercultural Services. Resources and Scholarships. Retrieved from http://studentaffairs.lmu.edu/interculturalism/ethnicinterculturalservices/eisoffices/chicanolatinostudentservices/resourcesscholarships/.

21. Georgetown University, Office of Undergraduate Admissions. International Applicants, Undocumented Students. http://uadmissions.georgetown.edu/applying-georgetown/international#UndocumentedStudents.

22. Saint Peter's University (2014). "Saint Peter's University Opens the Center for Undocumented Students," November 10, 2014. Retrieved from http://www.saintpeters.edu/news/2014/11/10/university-opens-the-center-for-undocumented-students/.

23. Fairfield University (2013). Center for Faith & Public Life. Immigration: Undocumented Students in Higher Education. Retrieved from http://www.fairfield.edu/academics/schoolscollegescenters/academiccenters/centerforfaithandpubliclife/researchscholarship/immigrantstudentproject/otherresources/.

24. Santa Clara University, Career Center. Resources for Undocumented Students. Retrieved from http://www.scu.edu/careercenter/students/findajob/ResourcesforStudents.cfm.

25. UCUS Report available online. Promoting Human Rights of Undocumented Students. Center for the Human Rights of Children, Loyola University Chicago. Retrieved from http://www.luc.edu/chrc/childrenandyouthnavigatingsystemsalone/promotinghumanrightsofundocumentedstudents/.

26. Student Diversity and Multicultural Affairs (SDMA), Student Life and Engagement Undocumented Student Resources. Retrieved from http://luc.edu/diversity/resources/undocumentedstudentresources/.

Conclusion

LAURA NICHOLS AND TERRY-ANN JONES

Combined, the chapters in this book provide perspectives on the individual experiences of students trying to overcome many odds to graduate from college, and the advocates, staff, and faculty who work within and around systems to help them during this politically fractious legal and historical period. This book adds to the rich historical and legal research and analysis on immigration in the U.S.[1] by specifically focusing on this history and policies as they relate to college students. The work in these pages also corroborates the findings of the small but growing body of research on the experiences of college students who are undocumented. In addition, this book provides an institutional perspective that considers the role of organizations as mediators between individuals and the social policies that are restricting their ability to operate as desired in following traditional paths of success in the United States.

The students' and universities' experiences expose current issues that allow us to more deeply think through the greater historical and structural realities of migration and the role of religious institutions in expanding global networks. Although the power and reach of religious institutions may be waning, especially in highly developed nations, their influence as long-standing entities with a global reach sets the stage to consider the role of such institutions in the lived experiences of recently migrated families, especially at a time when nationalist policies and political debates center around contentious issues associated with citizenship and immigration and often conflict with the extreme realities of global inequality and mass migration.[2]

The overarching conclusions that the authors drew from listening to students are that students struggle primarily with emotional stress related to their undocumented status, fear that they or their family members will be deported, the financial burden of attending college, and uncertainty regarding their futures. These forms of stress distinguish their college experiences from those of their peers who, despite having their own concerns, are more likely to have access to resources such as financial aid, medical insurance, or other basic privileges such as driving legally or having access to government-issued forms of identification. However, our analysis supports the perspective of Engebrigtsen, who cautions those studying the issue not to stop at the conclusion and "general proposition that child migration leads to psychological trauma."[3] It was not the migration process itself that necessarily created the greatest source of stress for students; rather it was the fear of the seemingly random differences by municipalities in the application of ad hoc deportation orders and the ambiguities in federal policy initiatives on which students' futures relied, combined with a college climate ignorant about immigration issues, that ultimately led to the most stress for students. These differences by state, with the federal government ultimately governing citizenship laws, also trapped staff and college administrators who were trying to understand and adhere to complex laws while at the same time trying to live up to their commitments to provide the same level of support and opportunity for undocumented and documented students alike.

Individual Experiences and Organizational Responses

Despite their additional emotional and economic burdens, undocumented immigrants tend to perform exceptionally well in college.[4] This may be because those who make it to college and receive funding or are financially able to attend are positively self-selected and possess the types of aptitude and ambition valued by educational institutions. Or perhaps, given their sacrifices and their families' sacrifices, they feel an exaggerated sense of obligation to excel. In either case, the career limitations they face upon graduating are even more tragic given their motivation and accomplishments. The students' characteristics, combined with the lack of structural opportunity, result in a unique opportunity to develop new policies for this particular subset of first-generation immigrants to the U.S.

Indeed, human and social capital are extremely important aspects of students' success and ability to navigate getting into and staying in college. Given that most students are also the first in their families to graduate from college, the same networks that supported their admission and matriculation remain necessary as they continue their lives and launch their careers following graduation. High school and college counselors and staff are crucial to students' success in navigating existing systems and providing emotional support and guidance. Thus, at the micro level the emphasis on *cura personalis* and educating the whole person that is ubiquitous in Jesuit education could be fully lived out for staff, faculty, and students in a mutually beneficial way, allowing staff to find fulfillment in being able to practice their personal missions and provide access to an educational system staff value highly to help advance students who rely on them as true allies.

From an organizational perspective, the greatest shortcomings within the colleges were the lack of explicit, consistent policies regarding admission of and support for students who were undocumented. The lack of transparency and financial support limited the number of students who managed to make their way through the nebulous channels. Furthermore, the absence of consistent policies and leadership that was often quiet on the issue left university staff in doubt regarding the legality of and support for their actions on behalf of students. On the other hand, our research demonstrated that the overwhelming majority of university personnel at Jesuit colleges were committed to supporting undocumented students to the extent that they could, illustrating their engagement with the missions that these institutions embrace. However, the absence of university policies and consistent practices pertaining to undocumented students left staff and students alike at the mercy of the will, knowledge, and practices at the individual level, risking students' well-being and their ability to continue as university students if those knowledgeable staff members leave the institution. As such, we strongly encourage institutions to institutionalize the current informal practices of individuals by making the support of undocumented students part of the job descriptions of some key staff members, advertising such support, and making sure staff and faculty training includes both information about the presence of undocumented students on campus and information about who on campus can help these students. In addition, we need more research at the organizational level about the strategies that staff use to accomplish institutional goals, when those goals conflict with federal laws and policies.

Finally, the student experiences gathered in this study provide guidance to higher education institutions about the potential barriers in educating students who are not only undocumented, but are also in many cases the first in their families to attend college, are low-income, and usually are members of racial and/or ethnic groups that are most likely to be under-represented on college campuses, especially at private colleges and universities. Thus the growing cost of college, combined with ongoing conflicts and politics around race in college, puts students who are undocumented in a particularly vulnerable position from which to pursue a degree. Cecilia González-Andrieu describes those students who make it to higher education at all as "the unlikely survivors of the convergence of economics and legislation that makes higher education one of the most unattainable of goals for many youth."[5]

Structural Realities in a Global Context

Even within the large network of Jesuit colleges and universities, individual staff, faculty, students, and institutions face limitations on what they can do to support undocumented students. At the most macro level, the patterned issues raised by students are also a reflection of the larger realities that nations and communities must face regarding immigration policy and are at the heart of policy conundrums. The fact that students' experiences with legal entities and threats of deportation differ depending on the state in which they grew up demonstrates the extremely diverse reactions and responses to undocumented immigrants in the U.S. on a state-by-state basis, despite the federal purview of immigration status.[6] Sharp cultural and political divisions on questions related to the value of new immigrants—who has access to the "American dream," rights, responsibilities, and deservedness[7]—are evident in the ambivalence and understanding of students who feel guilty for receiving scholarships and the opportunity for higher education. In addition, comments by students and faculty on campuses, even in formal venues such as the classroom, show the ignorance that exists among many about why individuals migrate, laws associated with achieving citizenship, and the fact that being undocumented is a civil, not a criminal offense.

While such ambiguities and hostilities are being played out on a national stage, larger global realities hamper the ability to adequately address these issues at a national level. As Sassen argues in *Expulsions*, the mass migration, displacement, and imprisonment of people around the world are part of the huge global forces that disconnect populations from each other and the earth.[8] Without a larger global body governing responses to mass migration, a question becomes whether an entity such as the worldwide Catholic Church can provide a level of leadership and international guidance.

Jacqueline Maria Hagan attests to the relationship between migration and faith. We share her argument that "religious institutions offer a unique vantage point on international migration because they transcend the boundaries of nation-states and often recognize migration as a fundamental human right."[9] Even if some Jesuit colleges and universities distance themselves from religious labels, their missions and identities reflect their commitment to social justice, and supporting undocumented students falls squarely within their purview. Although Hagan's study emphasizes migrants' connections to their faith rather than the role of religious institutions, her finding that undocumented immigrants identify their faith as a source of support in times of hardship reinforces what the authors of this book found in our study of undocumented students at Jesuit institutions: Students seek out both Jesuit institutions and religious leaders within their communities with the expectation that their commitment to their faith represents a commitment to help those in need. This inspires trust in Jesuit institutions and a sentiment on the part of the students and their parents that the institutions' missions and identities translate to a level of trustworthiness that far supersedes any trust they have in the state.

Contemporary immigrants are as deserving of the support and protection of Jesuit and Catholic institutions as nineteenth- and early-twentieth-century immigrants were. Schlichting's overview of the historical relationship between the immigrants and Jesuit institutions in Chapter 2 suggests that the Catholic Church was central to the acculturation of Catholic immigrants from European countries and contributed to the success of Irish- and Italian-Americans. In contrast, Portes and Rumbaut argue that Mexican-Americans, who comprise the largest immigrant group in the United States, and who are predominantly Catholic, are not granted the same level of support and accommodation that European immigrants received. Mexican-American youths, they argue, are underserved by the Catholic educational system.[10] The Catholic educational system's disproportionate support for European-descendant Catholics is evident in the geographic concentration of parochial schools on the East Coast and the Great Lakes regions of the United States, where early immigrant populations were concentrated. The presence of Catholic schools on the West Coast and in the Southwest, where there are large populations of Mexicans, Mexican-Americans, and other Central Americans, is marginal by contrast. Mexicans are not only the largest immigrant group in the United States, but they are also the fastest growing group of U.S. Catholics.[11] Still, their presence at Catholic educational institutions is not as pronounced as that of other groups. By contrast, the Catholic Church was quick to accommodate middle-class Cuban-Americans who arrived in Miami in the 1960s and 1970s by establishing schools and parishes to support their acculturation following their arrival during that period. Portes and Rumbaut note that, "nationwide, about one-quarter of children of Catholic families attend parochial schools today, while children of Latin American (mostly Mexican) families do so at the rate of only 4 percent."[12] Although an analysis of the reasons for the discrepancies in the Catholic educational system's support for and interaction with different ethnic and national groups is beyond the scope of this book, a consideration of Jesuit institutions' historical relationship with immigrants suggests that there is precedent for Jesuit institutions to not only advocate for immigrants, but to strive to support them using their institutional resources and influence on the larger society.

The Potential of a Network of Institutions

The influence of advocacy groups on social policy development and implementation is well researched, and grassroots groups have certainly mobilized to influence federal and state immigration policies.[13] Yet established formal institutions also can and do play a powerful role in guiding social policy. In this book we provide an example of one such network, the network of Jesuit universities and colleges. And while the research and focus presented here is U.S.-based, the Jesuit network of higher education is an international one. There are 189 Jesuit schools of higher learning throughout the world, and although the schools operate independently, more alliances are being made that connect institutions. For example, there are a growing number of study-abroad programs that have been formed to provide a Jesuit network of opportunities in Latin America and the Philippines for students from North America. Historically, Jesuit schools have provided an alternative education for Catholic

immigrants, and this tradition can continue if institutions choose to offer a positive response to the current mass migrations of peoples around
the world.

Examining the 1.5-generation of migrants brought to the U.S. as children
brings to light the contradictions in and struggles of legally educating undocumented K–12 students in public education while also enforcing laws
related to citizenship status in terms of travel and employment, with protections ending when students turn 18. In the case of this book in particular, the often-conflicting goals of religious institutions and government
entities are evident. The Catholic Church, being a global force, has a long
history of walking with and creating formal institutions such as churches
and schools in response to its followers migrating to different parts of the
world. In addition, the church flourishes in communities with new immigrants and is "dying" in those areas where new immigrants have not
replenished the generation of Catholics from Europe who arrived to the
U.S. in the late 1800s and early 1900s. While religious institutions must
follow the rules and laws of the states in which they operate, their values
(and interests) often lead them to see people as global citizens and to fight
for the dignity of the human person as a higher good than citizenship as
a marker of deservedness.

As Canaris remarks in Chapter 4, "Our research findings argue that if
the whole Jesuit network of higher education in the United States were to
become more fully engaged in the challenges and issues of undocumented
students, an engagement rooted in the history and principles of Ignatius
and his followers through the years, then other colleges and universities
could be emboldened with their own unique senses of mission and identity to exercise new models of leadership in related areas." We saw this in
practice in the state of California just after the conclusion of our study.
Most of the students we interviewed said that even community college
would have been out of financial reach for them. Their scholarship to a
Jesuit school was their only path to higher education. However, now for
students from California, the California DREAM Act[14] of 2011 allows state
aid to be granted to students who are undocumented and meet other
criteria. This is now true in a growing number of states.[15] Another law now
permits state schools in California to accept private scholarship money
for undocumented (classified in the state as AB540) students. Before this
time, private colleges in California had their pick of high-excelling students

who were undocumented, until state policy caught up to what private funding and private universities had already allowed.

Future Research with Students Who Are Undocumented in Higher Education

The uncertainty of the temporary status of DACA, along with widely varying views on immigration between and even within political parties at the federal level, means that colleges will likely continue to be mediators between degree-seeking students and federal legal restrictions. Thus college staff and administrations must continue to be aware of and consider the ways in which they will respond to students who are undocumented and seeking higher education. Institutions would do well to implement many of the policies and practices suggested by students and profiled in the institutional case study and formalize their efforts to support students. They should also make a greater effort to understand the barriers to the success of undocumented students, and the potentially positive effect of changing national policy and regulations.

At the federal level, networks such as the AJCU have the opportunity to provide leadership in terms of what serves the best interests of their network and ability to live out their mission as institutions of higher learning in the U.S. Right now, the ability of Jesuit schools to practice a mission of serving those most vulnerable is impeded by federal law, which puts staff at these institutions in the difficult position of trying to equally work for all students, when some cannot receive the same services and opportunities as students who are citizens.

Concluding Thoughts

Immigration policy and practice has long been an issue of intense debate in the United States, resulting in an ambiguity of stance and laws that causes negative lived realities for individuals. These outcomes are most readily evident when looking at the lives of undocumented immigrants of the 1.5 generation, those raised from a young age as North Americans and educated in U.S. school systems. The issues are even more profound when looking at those who have excelled and obtained admission to a U.S. college or university. These students have done everything "right" by cultural standards, but are suddenly denied access to institutions and structural legal protections when they become adults.

It is commendable that despite the limitations created by the informal nature of the process, that networks of students, faculty, and staff at Jesuit institutions in collaboration with high school teachers, guidance counselors, clergy, and other supporters, create the means by which undocumented students are able to gain access to tertiary education. The students and their families do their part to ensure student success through their relentless determination, their frugal use of resources, and their commitment to high academic standing despite the daily challenges that they face. Still, the success of the students who persevere to the point of obtaining bachelor and even graduate-level degrees should not incite complacency, as stories of student success serve as indicators of individual motivation rather than achievements on the part of institutions. Institutions need to continue to strive for policy changes that grant all students the right to access education at all levels. Even before policies change, private institutions in particular have the authority to create formal channels through which a greater number of undocumented students can gain access to higher education. Furthermore, many staff and faculty at Jesuit institutions believe they have the moral obligation to do so.

Notes

1. For example, Mae M. Ngai, *Impossible Subjects: Illegal Aliens and the Making of Modern America* (Princeton, N.J.: Princeton University Press, 2004).

2. Douglas S. Massey, Jorge Durand, and Nolan J. Malone, *Beyond Smoke and Mirrors: Mexican Immigration in an Era of Economic Integration* (New York: Russell Sage Foundation, 2002). Tanya Golash-Boza, *Immigration Nation: Raids, Detentions, and Deportations in Post-9/11 America* (London: Paradigm Publishers, 2012).

3. Ada Engebrigtsen, "The Child's—or the State's—Best Interests? An Examination of the Ways Immigration Officials Work with Unaccompanied Asylum Seeking Minors in Norway," *Child and Family Social Work* 8, no. 3 (2003): 196.

4. William Pérez, *Americans by Heart: Undocumented Latino Students and the Promise of Higher Education* (New York: Teachers College Press, 2012), 125.

5. Cecilia González-Andrieu, "The Good of Education: Accessibility, Economy, Class, and Power," in *Teaching Global Theologies*, ed. K. Pui-Lan, C. González-Andrieu, and D. N. Hopkins (Waco, Tex.: Baylor University Press, 2015), 60.

6. Monica W. Varsanyi, ed., *Taking Local Control: Immigration Policy and Activism in U.S. Cities and States* (Stanford, Calif.: Stanford University Press, 2010).

7. As discussed in: Ngai, *Impossible Subjects*; Selcuk R. Sirin and Michelle Fine, *Muslim American Youth: Understanding Hyphenated Identities through Multiple Methods* (New York: New York University Press, 2008).

8. Saskia Sassen, *Expulsions: Brutality and Complexity in the Global Economy* (Cambridge, Mass.: Harvard University Press, 2014).

9. Maria Hagan, *Migration Miracle: Faith, Hope, and Meaning on the Undocumented Journey* (Cambridge, Mass.: Harvard University Press, 2008), 8.

10. Alejandro Portes and Ruben G. Rumbaut, *Immigrant America: A Portrait* (Berkeley: University of California Press, 2014), 340.

11. Ibid.

12. Ibid.

13. Walter J. Nicholls, *The DREAMers: How the Undocumented Youth Movement Transformed the Immigrant Rights Debate* (Stanford, Calif.: Stanford University Press, 2013). Lisa (Leigh) Patel, *Youth Held at the Border: Immigration, Education, and the Politics of Inclusion* (New York: Teachers College Press, 2013). Gabriela Madera et al., eds., *Underground Undergrads: UCLA Undocumented Immigrant Students Speak Out* (Los Angeles, Calif.: UCLA Center for Labor Research and Education, 2008).

14. http://www.csac.ca.gov/dream_act.asp.

15. Anna Sampaio, *Terrorizing Latina/o Immigrants* (Philadelphia, Pa.: Temple University Press, 2015), 150–151.

Contributors

MICHAEL M. CANARIS is Assistant Professor of Ecclesiology at Loyola University Chicago's Institute of Pastoral Studies, teaching at both its Chicago and Rome campuses. He holds a PhD from Fordham University and has degrees from or has taught at six of the twenty-eight American Jesuit universities. He spent two years studying theological and interreligious responses to migrants and refugees in the UK and Italy. He was the administrative coordinator for the Ford Foundation grant while writing for this book.

MARIA D. GUZMÁN joined YMCA of the USA in February 2014 as a Program Evaluation Specialist. She co-developed the Undocumented Safe Space/Ally Training for Loyola University Chicago constituents. Dr. Guzmán graduated from Loyola University Chicago with a Doctorate of Philosophy and a Master of Arts in developmental psychology and a Bachelor of Science in psychology.

TERRY-ANN JONES is Associate Professor of Sociology and Anthropology and Director of International Studies at Fairfield University. Her research is focused on international migration, and she is the author of *Jamaican Immigrants in the United States and Canada: Race, Transnationalism, and Social Capital*.

SUZANNA KLAF is the Interim Director of Faculty Teaching Initiatives and Programs in the Center for Teaching and Learning (CTL) at Columbia University. She holds a PhD in Geography—Urban, Regional, and Global Studies from the Ohio State University, and an MA in Geography from Binghamton University (SUNY).

LAURA NICHOLS is Associate Professor of Sociology at Santa Clara University in California. Her work focuses on the application of sociology to program improvement and policy as well as inequalities and the experiences of first-generation college students.

MELISSA QUAN is Director of the Center for Faith and Public Life at Fairfield University, where she has worked since 2002. Quan completed her Master's degree in Education at Fairfield University in 2005 and is currently pursuing a doctoral degree in Higher Education Administration at the University of Massachusetts Boston.

KURT SCHLICHTING is the E. Gerald Corrigan '63 Chair in Humanities and Social Sciences and Professor of Sociology at Fairfield University. His research interests include the social history of New York and the city's immigrant neighborhoods. He is the author of *Grand Central Terminal: Railroads, Architecture, and Engineering in New York*, the basis for the PBS American Experience documentary *Grand Central*.

ANA NOBLEZA SISCAR practices immigration law at Ana Nobleza Siscar, LLC. Siscar earned an LL.M. degree from the University of Arizona as a Fulbright scholar. She has been admitted to the New York Bar and the Philippine Bar and has taught at Fairfield University and at Philippine law schools. She currently serves as an officer in the Connecticut American Immigration Lawyers Association.

KATHERINE KAUFKA WALTS is the Director of the Center for the Human Rights of Children at Loyola University Chicago. She received her JD from the University of Wisconsin-Madison. She is also a former immigration attorney and co-chairs Loyola's interdisciplinary "DREAMer Committee" of faculty, students, and staff dedicated to improving educational outcomes for undocumented students.

SAHNG-AH YOO is a graduate student studying Criminology and Criminal Justice at the University of Oxford, England. Having received her BA in psychology from Columbia University, her research interests are focused on applying the behavioral sciences to institutional policies and practices to better support human rights and social justice.

Acknowledgments

We acknowledge the courage of the students who allowed us to interview them. Many of them had never before discussed their status with people outside of their families. We are grateful to them and to their families for sharing their stories, without which this project would not have been possible.

We especially thank the staff, faculty, and administrators of the six institutions that were part of the in-depth case study for hosting us and sharing their experiences and practices. A special thanks is owed to Melissa Quan, who was the manager for all stages of the research project.

In addition to the contributors of this volume, there were many more colleagues who participated in bringing this project to fruition, including Cynthia Mertens; Philip Nyden; Bob Araujo, S.J.; Paul Roberts; Chris Kerr; and Nick Napolitano.

The research for this book was made possible with funding from the Ford Foundation. We would also like to acknowledge the support of Jeffrey P. von Arx, S.J., President of Fairfield University; Richard Ryscavage, S.J., Founder and Director of the Center for Faith and Public Life; and Noel Appel, former Associate Vice President for Advancement for their work in helping to secure this funding. We also thank Santa Clara University's Office of the Provost for covering the indexing costs of the book.

We thank the editors at Fordham University Press, especially Fredric Nachbaur, Will Cerbone, and Eric Newman as well as the Board of Directors, for publishing this body of work. Anonymous external reviewers provided extremely helpful comments and suggestions, which helped us to refine the chapters.

Terry-Ann thanks the family, friends, and colleagues whose support was instrumental to the completion of this project. Laura thanks friends and colleagues whose research and care for students has helped ground and guide this work.

Finally, we thank the contributors for creating this volume with us.

Index